Artifacts of Diplomacy:
Smithsonian Collections from
Commodore Matthew Perry's
Japan Expedition (1853–1854)

Chang-su Houchins

SMITHSONIAN INSTITUTION PRESS

Washington, D.C.

Library of Congress Cataloging-in-Publication Data
Houchins, Chang-su.
Artifacts of diplomacy : Smithsonian collections from Commodore Matthew Perry's Japan Expedition (1853–1854) /
    Chang-su Houchins.
p.   cm.—(Smithsonian contributions to anthropology ; no. 37)
Includes bibliographical references
1. Perry, Matthew Calbraith, 1794–1858—Ethnological collections—Catalogs.   2. United States Naval Expedition to
Japan, 1852–1854—Catalogs.   3. National Museum of Natural History (U.S.).   Dept. of Anthropology—Ethnological
collections—Catalogs.   4. Ethnological museums and collections—Washington (D.C.)—Catalogs.   5. Material culture—Japan—Catalogs.   6. Japan—Antiquities—Catalogs.
I. Title.   II. Series.
GN1.S54   no. 37   [GN36.U62W18]   301 s—dc20   [952'.025]   94-42474

ISBN 1-56098-538-0

∞   This publication is the trade edition of Smithsonian Contributions to Anthropology, 37.

Cover design by Kathleen Sims.   Images are identified on pp. 74 and 75, *infra*.

Contents

Introduction

The "artifacts of diplomacy" so admirably researched in this volume constitute the little-known incunabula of Japan–United States trade relations, i.e., the Japanese materials brought back from Commodore Matthew Perry's historic voyage to Japan. This study documents for the first time a group of artifacts whose individual origins and collective meaning often have been poorly understood. These "first offerings" of Japan, as Perry called them, were considered by Perry and his lieutenants to be a disappointing and mediocre lot, although some later scholars lavished praise on these presumed "Imperial" gifts that had been transferred to the Smithsonian Institution. Until Chang-su Houchins compiled this work, there was little to resolve such disparate opinions about the so-called "Perry Collection," for no one had undertaken the extraordinary detective work necessary to distinguish the collection's various components and to sort out the provenance of each item.

The original documentation for this collection, as for so many others, has been widely scattered. The objects themselves have been through a rather confusing set of administrative transfers. Sometimes the name of the caretaking branch of the Smithsonian Institution was changed, although the objects did not move. The very first list of Smithsonian ethnology accessions in our oldest ledger is a list of these artifacts from Japan. Registrarial problems are evident as early as this list, for the clerk accidentally included gifts received in 1857 from the King of Siam among the list of the Japanese accession! Subsequently, labels fell off, objects got renumbered, and names were changed. People looked at a cup with a cover and saw a dish and a bowl, then renumbered and renamed them again. In order to resolve these questions, the existing paper trail, in the form of internal Smithsonian documents as well as journals and other archival information from Perry's time, had to be examined. In addition, the collection could only be sorted out by examining it in its entirety, as Houchins has done here.

The study that has resulted is part of a wider recent effort, now underway within Asian ethnology collections at the Smithsonian, to reinterpret old anthropological collections in light of two components: what they tell about the culture that produced the artifacts, and what they tell about the collecting culture. The topic chosen for this study is one of great potential iconicity because of the historic nature of Perry's voyage. One can read conflicting evidence about initial United States–Japanese attitudes or the perceived importance of future trade, as expressed in these earliest exchanges of gifts. There is little premonition here of later developments that made the United States and Japan the two greatest powerhouses of world trade just over a century later. By contrast, the roughly contemporaneous gifts brought back from Thailand (Siam), some of which were inadvertently cataloged with Perry's artifacts in the first ledger, show the enormous importance Thailand's King Mongkut placed on gift-giving and diplomacy with America to help preserve through this alliance his kingdom's independence against encroaching European colonizers. Quite apart from the historic significance of Perry's collection, one can admire the foresight of the collectors, who supplemented materials they were given with the everyday handicrafts and personal objects available in the Japanese markets, and who later included such material in the Smithsonian transfer. Today, these objects constitute a unique snapshot of preindustrial Japan's technology.

In making such assessments it is important to keep in mind the boundaries of this study. Houchins has systematically tracked down the existing artifacts from Perry's expedition that are in the Smithsonian collections. This includes gifts given to Perry personally (which he correctly understood must be transferred to the government), return gifts given to the United States government by (or on behalf of) provincial leaders within Japan, and also objects purchased for the government by Perry and his crew members. This does not include natural history specimens (which were transferred to the Smithsonian separately), and it also does not include later diplomatic gifts conveyed during the First Japanese Mission (1860). Thus, Japanese historians might focus on those later gifts and on that later occasion as a delayed but complementary part of the gift-exchange initiated by Perry; but that component has been studied elsewhere.

In this book on the Japan Expedition artifacts, Houchins has used all the available evidence to separate purchases from gifts and to suggest the provenance and intended destination of each. She also has speculated on the criteria of selection involved, including her judgment that some of the collection may represent a "primitive example of market research." Although individual Perry objects have been discussed and illustrated elsewhere, this is the first comprehensive catalog of the collection. It also includes quite new information on some supplementary materials, such as the previously unpublished Dudley collection of prints and artifacts assembled on this voyage and donated in 1977 to the Smithsonian's Museum of American History. The data and illustrations Chang-su Houchins has assembled here will make accessible an important collection of preindustrial Japanese artifacts and will provide welcome new information for a continuing assessment of this historic cross-cultural contact.

Paul Michael Taylor
Curator of Asian Ethnology
Department of Anthropology
Smithsonian Institution

Acknowledgments

I am particularly grateful to Dr. William Fitzhugh, former chairman of the Department of Anthropology, who initiated the Smithsonian's Perry Collection catalog project in 1978. The members of the Department of Anthropology Publications Committee, namely William Fitzhugh, Ives Goddard, Ruth Selig, William Sturtevant, Douglas Ubelaker, Herman Viola, all of the National Museum of Natural History, and Felix Lowe, of the Smithsonian Institution Press, reviewed the first draft manuscript in early 1980 and made very useful critical comments and suggestions. The manuscript also was reviewed by Gordon Gibson, Adrienne Kaeppler, and Wilcomb Washburn. The firm guidance of Ives Goddard, William Sturtevant, and especially Paul Michael Taylor was extremely helpful at various stages of the project.

In recent years, a number of colleagues assisted me with expertise in their various areas of specialization. Although their family names are appropriately noted within the catalog's text, I extend special thanks to Tanabe Satoru, Chief Curator of Ethnology and Director, Yokosuka City Museum; Patricia Fiske, former Director of The Textile Museum, now Assistant Director of the National Museum of African Art; Amanda Stinchecum, Japanese textile specialist; Ann Yonemura and Louise Cort, The Freer and Sackler Galleries of Art; Okada Shigehiro, National Museum of Japanese History; Komatsu Taishu, Tokyo National Museum; Sahara Makoto, Nara National Research Institute of Cultural Properties; Gibo Eijirō, member of the Okinawa Cultural Properties Protection Committee; and Takako M. Hauge of Falls Church, Virginia, specialist in folk traditions in Japanese art. I am equally grateful to Katagiri Kazuo, Aoyama Gakuin University, and Honda Shozo, The Library of Congress, for their expert assistance in the interpretation of obscure terminology so often encountered in official documents of the Edo period.

I especially wish to express my gratitude to Georgia Reilly, Annamarie Rice, Barbara Watanabe, Johanna Humphrey, and Norman Wibowo for their assistance with the final draft of the manuscript, to Shobayashi Ikuko for preparing the Japanese script for printing, Marsha Bakry for stripping the Japanese script onto the camera-ready pages, Victor E. Krantz for photography, and James J. Cho for drawing the front cover illustration. Thanks also are due to Diane Tyler who edited and designed the monograph with great care.

Artifacts of Diplomacy: Smithsonian Collections from Commodore Matthew Perry's Japan Expedition (1853–1854)

Chang-su Houchins

Chronicle of the Perry Collection

Commodore Matthew Calbraith Perry's Japan Expedition, 1853–1854, was more than a successful diplomatic mission. Fortunately, the expedition also resulted in the introduction to the American people of a broad range of materials of lasting historical, ethnological, and scientific value. The Smithsonian collections of Japanese ethnographic artifacts, obtained by that memorable expedition, was the first major accession of ethnological materials by the United States National Museum (now the National Museum of Natural History, Smithsonian Institution) more than a century ago.[1] It has and, hopefully, will continue to serve as a body of primary data on the material culture of traditional or preindustrial Japan. It is precisely with this hope that the compilation of a catalog of the Perry collection was undertaken.

Although no record of Perry's pre-Japan Expedition connection with the Smithsonian Institution survives, his postexpedition contacts suggest that prior arrangements were made with Smithsonian officials for the collection of various specimens.[2] S. Wells Williams, Perry's chief interpreter, noted the Commodore's seriousness of purpose in the collection effort. Williams' diary entry for 26 July 1853, Naha, Ryūkyū, states that "the Commodore wished particularly to get a great variety of articles—silks, cottons, lacquered ware, china-ware and other products—to put in a museum in Washington."[3] At Perry's specific suggestion, Dr. James Morrow, the expedition agriculturist, purchased many samples of Japanese paper on 1

May 1854 at Shimoda.[4] The Commodore's active interest in acquiring materials persisted until the expedition's last few days in Japan, as evidenced in the final entry (23 June 1854) in Morrow's Japan journal.

I was ordered by Commodore Perry to pay Mr. Jones [Rev. George Jones] for some Japanese shrines [cf. catalog entries 77–79] and a few agricultural implements out of the fund of the Department of Interior[5] which I had in hand. ... The Commodore had bought the articles [via Mr. Jones] the day before, when on shore, at the Bazaar.[6]

Also noteworthy are the Smithsonian Institution annual reports for the years 1854 and 1855. Both include sections that emphasize the importance of the Japan Expedition's accomplishments. The 1854 report notes the activities of Perry and Dr. James Morrow in the natural history field, including their collections of plants, seeds, reptiles, fishes, and birds.[7] The 1855 report cites additional acquisitions: "Commodore Perry has returned to the States, bringing with him copious journals of the voyage, with numerous drawings, and many collections illustrating the natural products and manufactures of Japan."[8] The 1855 notice apparently refers to Perry's return to the United States in January 1855; the February arrival at Brooklyn, New York, of the stores ship *Lexington,* carrying on board numerous plants, fruits, and other natural history specimens, together with "articles of presents from the Emperor of Japan;" and the arrival of the frigate *Mississippi* in April, with literary and scientific materials. The *Lexington's* specimens were forwarded to Washington, D.C., from Annapolis, Maryland. Perry had directed the Commander of the *Lexington* to sail for Annapolis, for the purpose of landing and

Chang-su Houchins, Department of Anthropology, National Museum of Natural History, Smithsonian Institution, Washington, D.C. 20560.

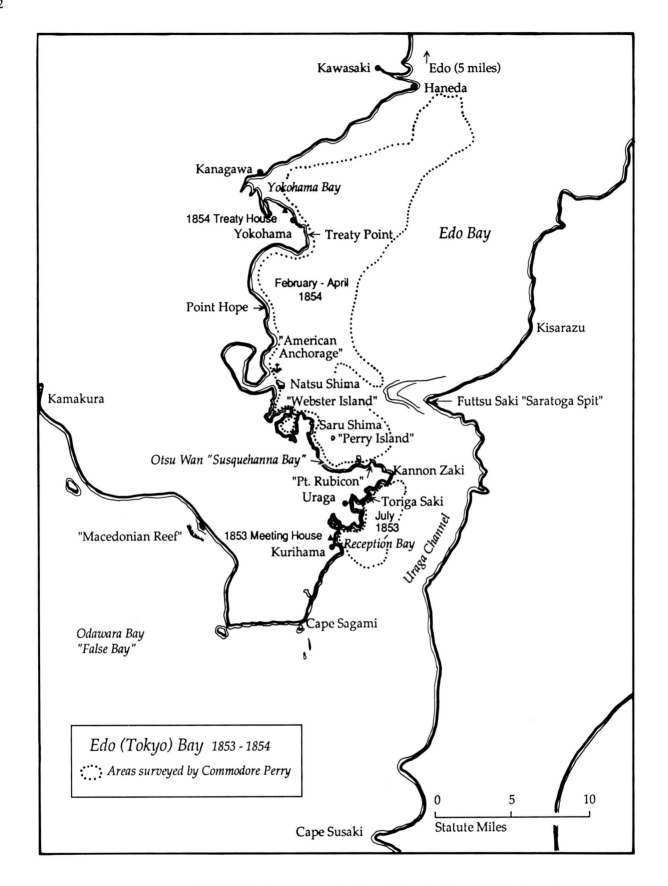

Edo (Tokyo) Bay, 1853–1854, showing areas surveyed by Perry. Redrawn from Pineau (1968, inside cover).

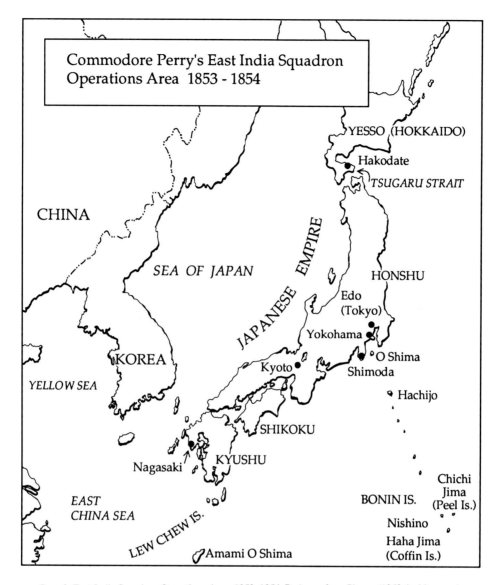

Perry's East India Squadron Operations Area, 1853–1854. Redrawn from Pineau (1968, inside cover).

transmitting her Japan cargo "with the least possible delay" to Washington.[9]

The natural history specimens, excluding the botanical materials, were delivered to the Smithsonian Institution between the spring of 1855 and the winter of 1856.[10] Several historians[11] have assumed that the Japan Expedition Ethnological collection was deposited at the Smithsonian Institution in the natural course of events; however, in late 1854 the final destination of the Japanese and Ryūkyūan gifts had yet to be determined. When the first group of Japanese formal gifts were boxed, labeled, and sent on board the stores ship *Supply* in 1854 for eventual forwarding to Washington, D.C., Perry left it to the Navy Department to decide "whether to forward them to the persons to whom they were given, or deposit them in the State Department, or sell them at auction for the benefit of the Treasury."[12] Perry had either dismissed his earlier intention of collecting various objects for "a museum in Washington,"[13] or had succumbed momentarily to his disenchantment with an array of objects he thought to be of little worth. Despite their lack of commercial value, the collections made by members of the naval expeditions were the lawful property of the United States government and were to be preserved and displayed in a national museum. Perry was well aware of these requirements.

Most of the ethnological materials are presumed to have been initially deposited at the Patent Office as part of the "National Museum," or more precisely stated, the "National Cabinet of Curiosities," and the remainder at the White House.[14] Although Perry informed the Secretary of the Navy that "various articles from the Emperor of Japan" were "mostly intended for the President's House,"[15] no record has yet been found of a large deposit at the White House. However, Muragaki Awaji-no-Kami (Lord of the Awaji district, modern Hyōgo prefecture), a senior member of the first Japanese Mission to the United States in 1860, records the Presidential reception given in the East Room of the White House on 17 May 1860.

In front of a large mirror, there was a table on which were displayed a lacquered writing box with *makie* [sprinkled or strewn gold or silver dust] decoration and several other ornate objects. We were told that they were the articles brought back from Japan by Perry.[16]

These objects probably were part of the Japanese items deposited at the Patent Office, which subsequently were transferred to the Smithsonian building. Most likely they were sent to the White House in preparation for that special occasion.

The Japan Expedition materials that the Japanese envoy saw displayed at the White House in 1860 may have included articles sent on the store ship *Supply,* after the expedition's first Japan visit in 1853. Perry's 5 September 1853 letter dispatched from Macao "to the President of the United States" is noteworthy.

Dear Sir, I send in by Lieut. Contee [Flag Lieutenant John Contee] a case containing the first offerings of Japan consisting of articles enumerated in the enclosed list.[17]

The list is missing, but, according to Williams' journal entry for 16 July 1853, two days after the delivery of President Millard Fillmore's letter of friendship and trade request to the Japanese officials, Kayama Eizaemon, the Governor [Assistant Magistrate] of Uraga brought "some presents" to Perry. They consisted of "5 pieces of brocade, 40 bamboo fans, 50 tobacco pipes and 50 lacquered cups."[18] In his memoir, the expedition artist William Heine also has an account of the event.

We received numerous gifts before we departed [Uraga]: fabrics (including gold brocade), over a thousand eggs, all sorts of lacquerware, saki, fans, and other things. The Commodore responded with gifts.[19]

Francis Hawks, author of the official narrative of Perry's Japan expedition, covers the event and gives rather superficial, yet lengthy, descriptions, without mentioning quantities of the various articles received.[20] It is doubtful that all 140 items were forwarded to the White House.

It was not until after 1857 that the Japan Expedition ethnological materials actually were incorporated into the Smithsonian Institution collections. In that year, the "National Museum" at the Patent Office was transferred to the custody of the Smithsonian Institution, in accordance with the law that provided that the Smithsonian would be the depository for "all objects of art and of foreign and curious, and all objects of natural history ... belonging to the United States which may be in the city of Washington," namely, the National Institute collections of the U.S. Exploring Expeditions, which also had been housed in the Patent Office, and other National Institute collections.[21]

The peregrinations of the Japan Expedition collection actually began in 1858, when it was removed from the Patent Office gallery to the newly completed Smithsonian building, where it formed the nucleus of the United States National Museum ethnology collections. It remained there for over two decades, under the direct care of then Assistant Secretary Spencer F. Baird, possibly with the assistance of John Varden. Varden had been in charge of the Japan Expedition materials at the Patent Office and was employed by the Smithsonian following the collection's transfer in 1858. The Varden diary entries for the entire month of June 1858 are monotonous recordings of his "packing and preparing to remove [the Patent Office collections] to the Smithsonian building." The first mention of the Japan Expedition collection at the Smithsonian appears in Varden's September 27th diary entry: "Jim [Campbell] cleaned case 82 for the Japan and Siam presents to the President of the United States."[22] In late 1858, Varden wrote that he "placed many of the specimens of Japan from the Emperor ... in case 82 and nailed the case up for the President."[23] It is not clear, however, whether the "nailing up" was done for the purpose of transporting the case to the White House or merely as a normal security measure. These may have been the specimens displayed at the White House for the Presidential reception honoring the Japanese Mission to the United States.

The first official Smithsonian record of the Japan Expedition ethnological collection is the Anthropology catalog book, number 1. Entry numbers 1 through 450 were made under the heading "Presents from the Emperor of Japan" and were dated March 9-12, 14, 1859. The catalog book was written in the hand of either Varden or an anonymous member of the staff. John Varden spent much of 10 March 1858 "at work arranging...[and numbering] specimens in the museum beginning on the N.W. gallery with the presents from the Emperor of Japan and Siam to Franklin Pearse [sic] President of the United States."[24] Varden's entering of "every specimen in its appropriate record book and the ineffaceable attachment of a number" is officially recorded in the Anthropology catalog book as having been "done by Mr. Varden for the ethnological collections."[25] It lists approximately 50 miscellaneous items from such other countries as Siam, the Philippines, and East India, along with several non-Perry Japanese specimens that were entered in error.[26] Therefore, the number of Japan Expedition items transferred from the Patent Office must have been approximately 400.

Following the formal establishment of the United States National Museum in 1876 and the 1881 reorganization of the Smithsonian Institution, the newly organized Department of Arts and Industries took custody of all ethnological materials, including the Japan Expedition collection. The National Museum building, now known as the Arts and Industries building, was completed in 1881. The Japanese ethnological collections were moved there at some point during the years 1882–1884, when a large number of specimens were removed from the Smithsonian building. Following the creation of the Department of Ethnology and the appointment of Professor

Otis T. Mason as its curator in 1884, all of the ethnological specimens of the museum were reported as being "under complete management."[27] More than a decade later in 1897, the Department of Anthropology was formed as a result of a general reorganization of the United States National Museum. It was then that the Japan Expedition collection was included in the department's Division of Ethnology collections, where it remains today. The wanderings of the Perry collection finally ceased when the National Museum of Natural History building was completed in 1911, and the collection has been housed there ever since.

The items listed in the Anthropology catalog book were not formally accessioned until August 1953, when the accession number 199043 was assigned. At that point in time, the total number of Japan Expedition ethnological items was given as 393, and they were cataloged as numbers 1 through 445 (cf. Appendix VI). The 5 August 1953 accession memorandum notes the complexity of the collection itself, its approaching centennial status, and states that the formal accession action was for the record only.[28]

A more recent Japan Expedition collection inventory, performed in 1969, superseded several earlier inventories and identified 203 items as Perry materials. It also restored the original catalog numbers by removing the new but duplicative numbers assigned in 1867. The 1969 inventory indicated that there were some 100-odd missing articles, including 19 specimens that already were noted as missing in the 1867 ledger. These were in addition to the printer's implements of seven plates [woodblocks], three brushes, one mallet, and a bottle of ink (catalog numbers 311–313), which had been part of the collections of the Division of Graphic Arts of the Department of Anthropology, but were transferred to the Department of the Arts and Industries in about 1920 and have remained unaccounted for ever since.[29] The 1867 recording may have been warranted by the Smithsonian building fire of 1865, which destroyed numerous objects from several early Smithsonian collections.[30] One traceable loss, a piece of silk, was faithfully reported by Varden. He wrote that he "took some cutting from the many duplicante [sic] pieces of silk, for handkerchief, for wipping [sic] specimens with...." To Varden, who spent two full weeks in September and October 1858 "cleaning and arranging" the Perry materials, the duplicate silk samples were useful conservation devices.[31]

The sheer number of items listed in various documents as either present or missing is, however, misleading. Many Japan Expedition specimens consist of several separate parts. Covered bowls, for example, frequently and inconsistently have been counted either as one or two items. Interestingly, when Perry compared articles received with accompanying lists, he readily discovered missing items just a day following formal receipt of the main portion of Japanese presents. His 31 March 1854 journal entry records that "on the following day [the presents] were examined and compared with the lists furnished, and a few articles were found to be missing abstracted probably by the Japanese servants."[32]

Although the apparent shrinkage of the collection may be alarming, it should be noted that several specimens presently missing are not necessarily lost. Several Japan Expedition objects have been lent to, or exchanged with, other institutions, both domestic and foreign. A sample of Ryūkyūan tobacco (catalog number 44) was sent to the Peabody Museum of Archaeology and Ethnology, Cambridge, Massachusetts, in 1877. A tobacco pouch and a pipe (catalog numbers 119, 120) went to an unidentified public school museum in New South Wales, Australia, in 1919, and, in 1928, one small bamboo basket and one rattan work basket (catalog numbers 109, 110) were sent to the Museum of Anthropology and Ethnography of the Academy of Sciences, Leningrad, Russia.[33] A "wood section" of an unidentified Japan Expedition object was formally condemned and destroyed in October 1971.

There are also those articles that have been separated from the original 1859 listings, prepared following the transfer from the Patent Office, as the result of internal transfers within the Smithsonian Institution. Several permanent transfers apparently were made for exhibit, conservation, and administrative purposes. In 1916, a total of 22 specimens, including textiles and decorated writing paper, were transferred to the former Department of Arts and Industries. This department was absorbed by the Department of Arts and Manufacturers in the Museum of History and Technology when the latter was founded in 1957, and these have been housed in that museum's Division of Textiles of the Department of Applied Arts, a unit newly organized in 1969.[34] But in 1979, the portion of decorated writing paper was returned to the original USNM ethnology collections.

Having reviewed several aspects of the history of the collection, perhaps more commonly known as "the Perry collection," it is necessary to correct fundamental errors in the initial descriptions of the Japan Expedition ethnographical materials. They were first listed as "Japanese presents from the Emperor of Japan" or "the Japanese Imperial gifts."[35] Some of them were indeed reciprocal gifts from the Japanese government, but neither the Emperor nor the Imperial household was involved. The return gifts were presented on behalf of the *Shōgun,* the chief of Japan's military government, some of his councilors, and reception commissioners. Furthermore, fully one-third of the materials in the collection were purchased with United States government funds by either Morrow, the expedition scientist, or Perry himself. A third category are those items that were given as personal gifts to Perry by either known or unspecified Japanese officials. According to Williams' journal, Perry received numerous gifts on his four separate visits to Naha between June 1853 and July 1854 (cf. Appendixes IIIA–IIID). Among the Ryūkyūan gifts were paper, cotton and silk fabrics, tobacco pipes and pouches, fans, lacquered articles, ceramics, and a temple bell. At Kanagawa, Shimoda, and Hakodate, in March–June 1854, Perry accepted such articles as swords, matchlocks, coins, silks, dresses, umbrellas, mats, lacquerware, shell-work, and a variety of other "little articles."[36]

6

Curiously, the Commodore's journal records neither the informal gifts he received nor the several objects he purchased, and his "List of Presents Received from the Emperor of Japan and His High Ministers for the Government of the United States and Others" (cf. Appendix II) is at variance with the official list (cf. Appendix I) as published in *Hawks Narrative*. When compared with the official list, Perry's private journal list includes either additional items and donors or a higher number of identical articles. But when compared with the Williams account and a Japanese document, "Jing'ei nikki" (records of the [Kanagawa] encampment), Perry omits such articles as gold and silver coins and misidentifies the donor of other items.[37] Williams reports that Perry received from Hayashi Noboru, chief reception commissioner, two swords, three matchlocks, and two sets of coins at Yokohama [Kanagawa] on 24 March 1854, but Perry lists only the swords and matchlocks as being the presents from the "Emperor."[38] According to the Japanese source cited above, the weapons and coins were presented by Hayashi at Perry's request. "Perry wanted these items for his government in Washington and the President of the United States."[39] Both sets of coins consisted of five different denominations in gold and silver. Hayashi also presented Perry with *The Points of a Horse*, a two-volume book authored by Hayashi, which contains a large number of colored woodblock illustrations. Perry was reported to have been impressed with their subdued coloring and the artist's realistic adherence to nature.[40] Lt. George Henry Preble reported that "among the presents received by Commodore Perry, was a box of obscene paintings of naked men and women."[41] At any rate, Perry did indeed accept several informal gifts.

Although seldom specific, Williams' journal also contains useful general information on the purchases of Japanese goods by Perry, his officers, and expedition sailors.[42] A number of expedition journals record the common complaint that the Commodore invariably asserted the privilege of making his own selections at the Shimoda, Hakodate, and Naha bazaars before any other members of the expedition had a chance to make their purchases. The lower ranking expedition members found the situation especially unfair. An account by the *Vandalia* cabin boy, W.B. Allen, of the bazaar held at a temple in Shimoda is vividly descriptive.

The things were got by lotery [sic]. You taking a ticket as you entered and upon entering the room you had a certain article marked on it which you immediately took if you liked it. ... I was rather unfortunate not drawing a single piece of lacqaware [sic] which I wanted very much. I suppose there was system of favoring going on for certain officers and for no one else.[43]

Available goods were lacquered bowls and boxes, cotton cloth, silk, hairpins, sashes, shoes, pipes, fans, coarse pottery, umbrellas, coarse baskets, and "items of Japanese art."[44] At Hakodate, Perry purchased an illustrated book for children, and his reaction to the art work was again favorable. He observed that as evidence of the advanced state of their art, Japanese artists demonstrated a knowledge of perspective and that they produced their works with unusual rapidity and dexterity. Perry witnessed the work of an artist employed by Rev. [George] Jones at Hakodate to paint a set of *byōbu* (folding screens).[45]

Kojima Matajirō, a Japanese shopkeeper who recorded the American expedition's Hakodate visit in his diary, which is accompanied by numerous drawings, is specific about the Commodore's and others' purchases. His 29 April 1854 diary entry reads:

Commodore Berori [Perry] made purchases at the store of Juhei Yamadaya: a fine lacquered box in tiers, a lacquered medicine case, brocade, and other things.

According to Kojima, the Americans bought, aside from such usual items as lacquerware, silks, and chinaware, ink and inkstones (cf. entry 126), children's parasols, tobacco pouches, wooden temple gongs, flower vases, wooden containers, chests of drawers, children's drums, and personal seals.[46] Dr. Morrow compiled lists of his purchases at both Shimoda and Hakodate during the period April to June 1854 (cf. Appendix IV).

Despite the 1858 Smithsonian annual report's accurate identification of the "collections of Commodore M.C. Perry, United States Navy, made while negotiating a treaty with Japan, and the presents to the United States government through him from the Japanese authorities,"[47] the erroneous "imperial gift" ascriptions have been perpetuated in all existing Smithsonian internal documents. One unhappy result of this misclassification is that such a distinguished historian as Samuel Eliot Morison also refers to the Smithsonian collection of Japan Expedition materials as "the Imperial gifts," although he correctly states that Perry received personal gifts that were subsequently deposited in the Smithsonian collections.[48]

The above survey of the informal or personal gifts accepted by Perry and of objects available for purchase[49] serves to establish the provenance of the bulk of the specimens assembled from unspecified sources. It provides a glimpse of Americans collecting abroad in a unique setting, which resulted in the earliest United States National Museum acquisition of Japanese ethnological materials. It also helps to compensate for several unfortunate characteristics of the Japan Expedition collection: sparsity of documentation, uneven sampling of artifacts, and overemphasis on exotica. It is apparent that the collection was made unsystematically, in the absence of field collection guidelines, and without such restrictions as locality, quality, and quantity. Furthermore, although the collection was intended for museum deposit, it was also a primitive exercise in market research; Perry, knowing President Fillmore's desire for trade, naturally was anxious to collect samples of Japanese goods marketable in America. Following the signing of the Kanagawa treaty for peace, amity, and commerce on 31 March 1854, Japanese officials allowed the Americans to purchase various items at shops and at the bazaars held at Hakodate and

Shimoda during April–June 1854. At Shimoda, authorities supplied a variety of goods in response to a list of the articles desired by the Americans (cf. Appendix V), which was prepared by the Japanese interpreters Moriyama Einosuke and Namura Gohachirō.[50] The reception commissioners' joint memorandum forwarding the list contains an apology for the inferior quality of some of the merchandise previously sold to the Americans during their first visit to Shimoda. The commissioners also expressed concern with the local scarcity of high quality articles desired by the Americans and the resultant difficulties in remedying the situation.[51] The items received as official return presents, on the other hand, reflect what the Japanese perceived to be representative cultural products and were felt by them to be barely suitable for presentation to a foreign government. They also subtly reflect Japanese perceptions, or misperceptions, of American or Westerner's wants and tastes.

A brief review of the initial reactions to the Japanese official gifts by Perry and other members of the expedition party, as well as subsequent assessments by modern historians, adds another dimension to the uniqueness of the Japanese Expedition ethnological collection. The first and lesser-known Japan Expedition gift exchange took place at Naha in June 1853. Perry presented his gifts to the Queen Dowager, Regent, and Treasurers of the Ryūkyū Kingdom on 7 June (cf. Appendix VIII). The following day, the Ryūkyūan return gifts of paper, cloth, tobacco, fans, tobacco pipes, and lacquerware (cf. Appendixes IIIA, IIIC) were delivered to Perry. Neither Perry's private journal nor *Hawks Narrative* reports the event. But Williams' journal entry for 8 June lists the articles received with the comment that they were "a trumpery assortment with a few pieces of lackered ware." Some of these items are presumed to be included in the Smithsonian collection, but one cannot be certain because Perry purchased similar objects at Naha on his first visit there.[52]

The second, less-formal gift exchange occurred at Edo Bay on 16 July 1853, as has been noted previously in connection with the earlier deposit of Perry-related objects at the White House. Although Kayama, the bearer of the presents, insisted that they were his own "personal favors," Perry quite properly declined to accept them as personal gifts from Kayama. Perry's judgment was correct: Kayama had merely carried out the *rōjū*'s[53] decision to "give the foreigners the articles they wanted to put off sending an answer to the [President Fillmore's] letter."[54] Perry forwarded them to the President as "the first offerings of Japan," adding that

they are of little value, but may be acceptable as coming from a country which has of late excited so much interest ... these are not by any means the best specimens of the work of the Japanese; with their usual duplicity they have doubtless kept the bulk of their finer products.[55]

Perry was not impressed with Kayama's "trifling presents," but was pleased with having established the precedent of gift exchange (cf. Appendix VIII), a form of "reciprocity of courtesy."[56] In the official *Hawks Narrative,* they were described as interesting specimens of Japanese manufactures, which were "credible evidences of mechanical skill," and whose "ornamental figures ... [showed] the grotesque fancy of Japanese art."[57] According to Bayard Taylor (1859),

They brought a number of presents, as souvenirs of our visit ... [the] fans [were] covered with hideously distorted and lackadaisical pictures of Japanese ladies[58] (cf. catalog entries 53–57).

On 24 March 1854, at Kanagawa, the most celebrated "Japanese presents" were formally received by Perry on behalf of the government of the United States, himself, and a few selected members of his squadron. The presents (cf. Appendixes I, II) were displayed on benches inside the large audience hall, and the reception commissioners stood in a line abreast at the head of the audience hall, while "the chief interpreter called off from written lists the several presents, by whom presented, and for whom intended.[59] Lt. George Henry Preble, who was detailed to escort the Commodore ashore to receive the Japanese presents, observed that the Commodore was received with more pomp and ceremony than on any previous occasion. Preble gives detailed descriptions of the articles received, along with his personal and others' reactions to them, including Perry's.[60]

Perry thought that the lacquerware, silks, and other presents were of no great value. His disappointment must have been obvious. The Japanese officials were moved to explain that they "had not had time to prepare more suitable gifts" and assured him that additional articles would be forthcoming. As a result, Perry wrote:

Before my departure from Shimoda, a collection better corresponding with those I had given would be provided.[61]

To Preble, the assembled presents formed a "pretty display," but were "of not much value." He remarked further that

[They were] not worth over one thousand dollars some thought. I am sure one of our presents of Audubon's Great Work on American birds was worth more than all we saw there, and our miniature railroad engine and car cost several times their value. Everyone, the Commodore included, remarked on the meagre display and the lack of rich brocades and magnificent things always associated with our ideas of Japan ... when exhibited in the U.S. I think these presents will prove a great disappointment to our people, whose ideas of Japan have been so exaggerated.[62]

Preble's additional comments are of interest to both historians and ethnologists:

It is to be regretted they do not include some of the rich brocades for which Japan is famed or any of their beautiful copper castings, or inlaid work of gold or silver ... something also that would illustrate the daily life and habits of a people excluded from the rest of the world so many years. The supposition of their magnificence and immense wealth, will I think prove a mistake. And the splendor of their court exists only in the romances of the old travellers and Jesuits.[63]

According to the report of Edward Yorke McCauley, Acting Master on the *Powhatan,*

The Japanese presents consisted of lacquered wares, crapes, silks, etc., but nothing very remarkable, or which could not be produced superior in the United States.[64]

Contrary to those who shared Perry's disappointment with the commonness and meagerness of the Japanese reciprocal gifts, others, including Williams, reacted favorably. Williams reported:

[They] were spread out on the mats, lying in pretty trays, and making a pretty show in consequence, far more than ours did ... [ours] were in brown paper and rough boxes.[65]

Referring to the quality of the articles displayed, he wrote that the articles were

of rarity of Japanese manufactures. ... some of the pieces of lacquered ware in raised gold figures were beautiful, and the silks rather fine, especially the heavy crapes; the pattern of which quite unlike anything made elsewhere.[66]

Williams was not alone in finding the display of the Japanese presents and their quality superior to the manufactures of other nations. Midshipman John Glendy Sproston observed:

The first objects that attracted my attention were lacquered boxes of different sizes and shapes, embracing several varieties of style ... their quality was evidently very superior and beautiful, evidently excelling every other nation ... of more beautiful varieties, no other nation can produce them.[67]

Dr. Morrow was realistically neutral:

Some of them were very fine, though the number was not large nor the aggregate value very great.[68]

Although a few of the expedition members' initial reactions to the Japanese return gifts were overwhelmingly negative, the overall assessments made by historians at a later date tend to be more generous and much less specific. Perry's early biographer, William Griffis, evaluated the presents as "delicate specimens" by Japanese artisans.[69] Robert Tomes, who prepared the abridgement of the official *Hawks Narrative,* implied American generosity (cf. Appendix VII) when he stated that "the Japanese were not to be outdone in generosity of articles of the manufactures of their country as return gifts."[70] Oliver Statler simply states that "a lavish exchange of gifts" took place between the American and the Japanese governments.[71] It is evident that the additional articles presented at Shimoda in June 1854 (cf. Appendix III) considerably altered the American evaluation of the Japanese return gifts. The less-critical opinions expressed over the years probably are indicative of improved American appreciation of Japanese arts and crafts. Morison's recent, and probably definitive, biography of Perry contains a brief passage describing the Japanese return gifts, together with Morison's assessment:

The imperial gifts ... are not worthy examples of Japanese art. The best are a brazen gong, two gold-lacquered boxes, a lacquered writing set, and about twenty bolts of silk ... many of the gifts are of coarsest sort. The entire lot could not have cost the *Bakufu* more than a few hundred *ryō.*[72]

It is doubtful that Morison examined in their entirety the articles included in the Japanese gifts presented at Kanagawa in March 1854 and the additional items delivered at Shimoda in June. Some of the best specimens of Japanese manufactures, such as the blue and white Imari porcelain pieces received at Shimoda,[73] are missing from his list. Yet, his monetary evaluation is realistic. The bankrupt *Bakufu* government, with its preindustrial economy and in the face of national crisis, was in no position to reciprocate in value the American gifts (cf. Appendix VII).

The second group of Japanese gifts was presented to Perry by the reception commissioners at the Ryōsenji, a temple in Shimoda, on 9 June 1854.[74] The Shimoda presents were clearly superior to the earlier ones. Hawks wrote that they were "handsome gifts ... [consisting of] some choice articles of Japanese manufacture."[75] Williams also was impressed. He thought that they were "fine specimens of manufacture ... and fully equal" in value to the American gifts.[76] Although Williams lists only a few sample articles, such as mats, dresses, and shellwork, the Japanese record (cf. Appendix III) lists some 30 varieties of articles, including the polearms decorated with inlaid mother-of-pearl and gilt metal work (entries 95, 96), large blue and white Imari porcelain vessels (entries 43–46), and lacquerware. According to a contemporary Japanese specialist, the Shimoda presents were a group of "carefully selected, elegant Japanese manufactures."[77] A special viewing of the additional presents to the President of the United States was held on 21 June, a few days prior to the American expedition's departure for home.[78]

The final, and least-known, exchange of gifts took place early in the homeward voyage. The occasion was the conclusion, on 11 July 1854, of treaty negotiations at Naha with the Ryūkyūan Kingdom. The Ryūkyūan gifts consisted of a large temple bell, pipes, cups, jars, cloth, and other produce.[79] But a Japanese language list, which was recorded by a Satsuma *han*[80] official stationed at Naha, contains a total of approximately 50 items in 17 varieties (Appendixes IIIB, IIID). The large bronze Gokoku-ji temple bell was cast by a Japanese metalworker in 1456 for King Shō Tai-kyū, who reigned from 1454 to 1461. The inscriptions on the bell have been reported to read: "Daiku Emon-no-jō Fujiwara Kunimitsu" (The [Japanese] Imperial Official Master Metalworker, Fujiwara Kunimitsu); "Keitai shichi-sai" (the seventh year of the Ming dynasty Ching t'ai period [1456]), along with a lengthy votive epitaph. In translation it is said to read in part:

May the sound of this bell shatter illusory dreams, perfect the souls of mankind, and enable the King and his subjects to live so virtuously that barbarians will find no occasion to invade the kingdom.

Upon Perry's explicit request, the Regent of the Ryūkyūan Kingdom presented the bell to the Commodore. Curiously, the temple bell does not appear in the list.[81] Only a few of these articles have survived. Perishables, such as rice, wine, fowl, eggs, sheep, and pigs, as well as the botanical specimens and the plant seeds, are excluded from the above descriptions of Japanese gifts. Also excluded are the three large pieces of stone received at Hakodate, Shimoda, and Naha, which were in response to Perry's specific request for them for the Washington Monument, and the three spaniels for President Pierce. The stone from Shimoda is said to have been built into the 202nd level of the monument and bears an inscription that records its origin;[82] however, U.S. Park Service records show that the Shimoda stone was built into the 220-foot-level and the Okinawa stone was put into the 210-foot-level.

Although the Japan Expedition materials in the Smithsonian collections often have been cited as highly prized, they seldom have been exhibited to the public. The earliest showing was in May 1860, when a limited number of specimens were viewed in the East Room of the White House at a reception honoring the members of the first Japanese Mission. Some members recall that they saw "large mirrors on all the walls, and before them, tables of various sizes, on which were placed Japanese lacquered writing boxes and other articles, which had been presented to Commodore Perry on his visit to Japan."[83] In the following month, five senior members of the mission, accompanied by two interpreters, visited the Smithsonian Institution, where Secretary Joseph Henry showed the guests various Japan Expedition articles, including a "collection of animals, birds, fishes, reptiles, and other curiosities."[84] It is not clear, however, whether the objects shown on that occasion were on display in the exhibit hall, or were merely arranged temporarily for viewing by the special visitors.

It was not until 1968 that a major exhibition of the Japan Expedition was held for a wider audience. More than thirty ethnological specimens[85] were shown in the National Museum of Natural History, along with numerous items assembled from non-Smithsonian sources, emphasizing the Commodore's personal role and accomplishments. In 1969, 36 artifacts, including lacquerware, pottery, kitchen utensils, carpenters' tools, and agricultural implements, were shown as part of a Japan Expedition exhibit by the Japan Society at Japan House, New York City. The Japan House exhibition presented a broad-ranging sample of the Japan Expedition ethnological materials. A small group of Japan Expedition materials (a total of eight items), including a fan, lacquered box, bamboo canteen, shell spoon, draw knife, compass saw, carpenter's plane, and an umbrella, were shown at the Naval Historical Foundation's Truxtun Decatur Naval Museum in Washington, D.C., during 1975–1976. Supplemented by a few Japan Expedition graphics, the exhibit unit was titled "Perry's Journey to Japan"; it formed a major part of the "Men Who Made the Navy" exhibit. The National Portrait Gallery included several lacquered objects and picture fans in its modest "Mission to Japan" exhibit of 1978. A lacquered, decorated inkstone box (catalog number 72) containing an inkstone, together with a water-dropper, a writing brush, a gimlet, and paper was shown at an exhibit, "Writing and Reading," organized by the Cooper Hewitt Museum of Decorative Arts and Design in New York City, 15 September 1981–3 January 1982. For the past several years a lacquered writing box, a ceramic cake box, and a sword and scabbard (catalog numbers 71, 107, 115, 116) were on view in the permanent exhibit of the Division of Naval History, National Museum of History and Technology. In October 1980, the unit was renamed the Division of Armed Forces History, National Museum of American History.[86]

Miscellaneous related materials, in addition to the National Museum Japan Expedition ethnology collection materials, have been chosen for inclusion in this catalog. The additional items are a small selection from the National Anthropological Archives print collections and Japanese objects from the Thomas C. Dudley collection, a recent acquisition of the Museum of American History's Division of Armed Forces History. The Anthropology archives holdings of five original drawings by an anonymous artist portraying Japanese, Ainu, and Ryūkyūan figures in native costume were formerly part of the National Museum ethnology collection. They were received from an unspecified source some time between 1908 and 1935, during which period Walter Hough was acting and subsequently head curator of the Department of Anthropology. Hough's handwritten annotations, signed "W.H.," on the reverse of each drawing read: "Sketch made by a naval officer in Japan apparently with the Perry Expedition." They possibly were accompanied by a photographic print of the painting of a Japanese village scene by William Heine, the expedition's principal artist, which was donated by the artist himself, certainly prior to his death in 1885. A signed notation on the reverse of the photo mount, reads in part: "The illustrations in my work are about four times this size." One can speculate that it was Heine's expressed wish either to sell or donate some of his unpublished works relating to the Japan Expedition. At any rate, the drawings and the photographic print described above were transferred to the archives' original print and photograph collections in 1965, following the organization of the archives unit within the Department of Anthropology.

The Dudley collection was received from his descendant, Eugenie M. Guilmette of Yonkers, New York, in 1977. Thomas C. Dudley was "purser's clerk on Commodore Matthew Perry's flagship, the Powhatan."[87] The Dudley collection consists chiefly of his personal effects and miscellaneous objects acquired during the years 1846–1855 in East India, China, and Japan, totaling 161 items.[88] Eleven Japan-related objects have been selected for inclusion to supplement and enhance the first Smithsonian collection of Japan Expedition ethnological materials.

Notes

[1]An earlier but minor accession of Japanese objects consisted of an assortment of 15 miscellaneous items (USNM Ethnology catalog numbers 3914–3918, 3922–3925, 3927, 3931, 5796–5799) collected by Charles S. Wilkes in Honolulu, 1840, during his expedition of 1838–1842. They were received from Japanese sailors who had been shipwrecked off the Sandwich Islands.

[2]For Perry's postexpedition correspondence relative to the deposit and mounting of bird specimens, see Perry letter of 3 November 1855 to Assistant Secretary Spencer F. Baird and Perry letters of 2 and 25 October 1856 to Secretary Joseph Henry, Smithsonian Institution Archives, Record Unit 52, United States Explorations and Government Reports, 1852–1860 (MS). Hereafter, these records will be referred to as SI Archives.

[3]S. Wells Williams, "A Journal of the Perry Expedition to Japan (1853–1854)," edited by F.W. Williams, *Transactions of the Asiatic Society of Japan*, 37(2)(1910), page 72. Hereafter, this will be referred to as *Williams Journal*. Perry's "museum" is a reference to the Patent Office galleries where the National Institute collections of objects of foreign origin were housed, and which had been officially designated in 1846 as the National Cabinet of Curiosities. See G. Brown Goode, "The Genesis of the National Museum." In *The U.S. National Museum Annual Report for 1891* (Washington, D.C., 1892), page 301.

[4]Allan B. Cole, editor, *A Scientist with Perry in Japan: The Journal of Dr. James Morrow* (Chapel Hill, North Carolina, 1947), page 172. Hereafter, this will be referred to as *Morrow Journal*.

[5]Dr. James Morrow was authorized by the Secretary of the Interior and apparently was provided with funds for the purpose of collecting seeds, plants, and other items during the visit of the East India Squadron to Japan. See Cole's introduction to *Morrow Journal*.

[6]*Morrow Journal*, page 203, for a reference to one of the several bazaars held in Shimoda.

[7]*Smithsonian Institution Annual Report for 1854* (Washington, D.C., 1854), page 9. Hereafter, all Smithsonian Institution annual reports will be referred to as *SI-AR* followed by the appropriate year.

[8]*SI-AR 1855*, page 47.

[9]Samuel Eliot Morison, *"Old Bruin" Commodore Matthew Calbraith Perry, 1794–1856* (Boston and Toronto, 1967), pages 415–416, 421. For the *Lexington's* cargo manifest, see Perry's letter of 9 October 1854 to the Secretary of the Navy, printed in "Correspondence Relative to the Naval Expedition to Japan," in 33rd Congress, 2nd Session, *Senate Executive Document 34*, serial 751, page 183.

[10]*SI-AR 1856*, page 62.

[11]For example: William Elliot Griffis, *Matthew Calbraith Perry: A Typical American Naval Officer* (Boston and New York, 1890), page 369; Cole's introduction to *Morrow Journal*, page xxi; Clay Lancaster, *The Japanese Influence in America* (New York, 1963), page 19; Morison, *Old Bruin*, page 424.

[12]Roger Pineau, editor, *The Japan Expedition 1852–1854; The Personal Journal of Commodore Matthew C. Perry* (Washington, D.C., 1968), page 194. Hereafter, this will be referred to as *Perry Journal*. According to William Speiden, Jr., Perry's purser, the "Commodore ordered the rice to be sent on board the *Supply* and the other articles to the *Powhatan*," 24 March 1854 entry in the unpublished journal of William Speiden, Jr., titled Journal of a Cruise in the U.S. Steam Frigate *Mississippi*, 1852–1855. The journal is held at the Naval Historical Foundation, located at the Navy Yard, Washington, D.C. (MS). Hereafter this will be referred to as Speiden Journal.

[13]*Williams Journal*, page 72.

[14]A bill for the preservation of collections of natural curiosities furnished by the exploring squadrons, and for investing the custody of the specimens in the National Institute was passed on 27 July 1842. See Goode, "Genesis," pages 310–318. The National Institute was established as the National Institution for the Promotion of Science and the Useful Arts in 1840. The name was changed in 1842, and the institute was dissolved in 1862 when its charter expired, ibid., pages 273–274, 293. When the Smithsonian Institution was established in 1846 the Patent Office collection was officially designated as the "National Cabinet of Curiosities." According to Goode, "Genesis," pages 301–302, 341, the term "National Museum" was not used between 1847 and 1851. After 1851, however, "National Museum" was used synonymously with the "National Cabinet of Curiosities." Secretary Joseph Henry of the Smithsonian Institution made the first public use of the term "National Museum" in 1855.

[15]Perry's letter to the Secretary of the Navy, 9 October 1854, in "Correspondence Relative to Naval Expedition," page 183.

[16]See Muragaki's diary entry for 17 May 1860 in Tanaka Kazusada, compiler, *Man'en gannen kem-bei shisetsu zuroku* [Pictorial Record of the 1860 First Japanese Embassy to America] (Tokyo, 1920), unpaginated.

[17]Perry letter of 5 September 1853, Macao, to the President of the United States, deposited in the Henry E. Huntington Library and Botanical Art Collection, 1151 Oxford Road, San Marino, CA 91108 (MS).

[18]*Williams Journal*, pages 67–68.

[19]William Heine, *With Perry to Japan, A Memoir by William Heine; Translated, with an Introduction and Annotations, by Frederic Trautmann* (Honolulu, 1990), page 75. Hereafter, this will be referred to as *Heine Memoir*.

[20]Francis L. Hawks, *Narrative of the Expedition of an American Squadron to the China Seas and Japan, Performed in the Years 1852, 1853, and 1854 under the Command of Commodore M.C. Perry...* (New York, 1856), pages 312–313. Hereafter, this will be referred to as *Hawks Narrative*. In *Hawks Narrative*, pages 262–272, Kayama is identified as "a Japanese official who spoke Dutch," and added to the items received was "mild tobacco." See also J. Willet Spaulding, *The Japan Expedition; Japan and Around the World, an Account of Three Visits to the Japanese Empire* (New York, 1855), page 169. Hereafter, this will be referred to as *Spaulding Journal*. For another account of the event, see also the 16 July 1854 entry in Speiden Journal.

[21]See especially Sections 5 and 6 of the final bill passed to establish the Smithsonian Institution, in *Proceedings of the 29th Congress, 1845–1846*, which was reprinted in William J. Rhees, editor, "The Smithsonian Institution: Documents Relative to its Origin and History," *Smithsonian Miscellaneous Collections*, number 328 (Washington, D.C., 1879), pages 471–472. See also *SI-AR 1857*, page 14 and Goode, "Genesis," pages 340–346.

[22]See Varden diary 1857–1863, included in Varden Papers, 1829–1863, Record Unit 7063, SI Archives (MS). Hereafter, these will be referred to as Varden Papers. See also *SI-AR 1858*, pages 53, 56.

[23]Varden's 2 October 1858 diary entry, Varden Papers.

[24]Varden's 10 March 1858 diary entry, Varden Papers.

[25]Catalog book number 1 is currently in the files of the Department of Anthropology Processing Laboratory. A close comparison with Varden's handwriting suggests that the catalog book is a copy of the 1858 original, reported in *SI-AR 1858*, page 56 as having been completed.

[26]Three items, catalog numbers 322–324, identified as "copper pan in lacquer stand" [braziers] definitely are known to be the presents to President James Buchanan brought by the first (1860) Japanese mission to the United States. See Kazusada, *Man'en gannen kem-bei shisetsu...*, which lists and illustrates these three objects. See also Madoka Kanai, *Man'en gannen kem-bei shisetsu shiryō shūsei* (Tokyo, 1961), volume 6, page 29, for another list that includes these three items, *"makie hibachi mittsu."* This raises a question as to the accuracy of the dates entered in the catalog book. Consider also the articles temporarily deposited at the White House; these could not have been transferred to the Smithsonian Institution until after May 1860.

[27]For changing status of ethnological materials, see *SI-AR 1883*, page 51; *SI-AR 1884*, page 57.

[28]For accession memoranda and other historical facts regarding the collection, see the National Museum of Natural History Registrar's Office, accession number 199043. Hereafter, the National Museum of Natural History will be referred to as NMNH.

[29]Ibid.

[30]For an account of the Smithsonian fire of 24 January 1865 and resultant losses, see Goode, "Genesis," pages 273–274.

[31]See 14 October 1858 diary entry, Varden Papers, for the episode of cutting a piece of silk.

[32]*Perry Journal,* page 194.

[33]Records of early exchanges are missing. For partial information, see the ethnology collection card catalog. Identification of articles received in exchange are not recorded. The exchange program with the Museum of Anthropology and Ethnography of the Academy of Sciences, Leningrad, was initiated in 1928. See NMNH Registrar's Office, accession number 103666. According to the Peabody Museum records, the Japanese tobacco sample (*Nicotiana tabacum*) given to them by the Smithsonian is still in their collection, and its catalog number is 77-36-60/12945. See Collection Administrator Sally Bond's letter of 8 October 1982 to Paul M. Taylor, Department of Anthropology, NMNH. As for the two baskets sent in 1928 to the Museum of Anthropology and Ethnography of the Academy of Sciences, Leningrad, Russia, they are presumably still in their collections. NMNH former director, Richard S. Fiske's letter of inquiry sent on 4 October 1982 received no response. The Bond letter and a copy of the Fiske letter are in the NMNH Registrar's Office, accession number 199043.

[34]The intramural transfer records are in the NMNH Registrar's Office, accession number 199043. The Department of Anthropology Accessions Committee approved the intramural transfer from the Museum of History and Technology to the NMNH on 23 October 1979. In October 1980, the name of the Museum of History and Technology was changed to the National Museum of American History.

[35]See, for example, anthropology catalog book, 1859; NMNH Registrar's Office accession number 199043; Perry letter to the Secretary of the Navy, 9 October 1854, in "Correspondence Relative to Naval Expedition," page 183; Morison, *Old Bruin,* page 424; Oliver Statler, *The Black Ship Scroll* (San Francisco, 1963), page 29.

[36]Regarding the U.S. government funds that were provided for purchasing objects, see Cole's introduction to *Morrow Journal;* also *Morrow Journal,* page 23 and *Williams Journal,* page 72. See *Williams Journal,* pages 24, 46, and 82 for dates and types of the informal gifts received at Naha, and pages 148, 158, 197–198, 205–206, and 215–216 for the informal Japanese gifts.

[37]For a close comparison of the respective lists, see *Perry Journal,* pages 195–196 and *Hawks Narrative,* pages 429–430.

[38]*Williams Journal,* page 148.

[39]"Jing'ei nikki" [Records of the (Kanagawa) Encampment], in *Bakumatsu gaikoku kankei monjo* (Tokyo, 1930), volume 5, pages 306–307, and cited in Tomio Hora, *Peri Nihon ensei zuikō-ki* (Tokyo, 1970), page 246, for conflicting reports on the coins.

[40]See *Hawks Narrative,* page 528, regarding the book Perry received and his reaction to it.

[41]For Preble diary entry for 25 February 1854, see Boleslaw Szczezniak, editor, *The Opening of Japan, A Diary of Discovery in the Far East, 1853–1856* (Norman, Oklahoma, 1962), page 126. Hereafter, this will be referred to as *Preble Diary.*

[42]*Williams Journal,* pages 78, 82, 246, and 248 for Ryūkyū, and pages 193, 195, 216–217 for Japan.

[43]W.B. Allen's 2 May 1854 diary entry in Henry F. Graff, editor, *Blue-jackets with Perry in Japan, the Diaries of Master's Mate J.R.C. Lewis of Macedonia and Cabin Boy W.B. Allen of Vandalia* (New York, 1952), page 154.

[44]*Williams Journal,* page 82; Hora, 1962:751.

[45]*Hawks Narrative,* pages 528–529.

[46]Matajirō Kojima, *Amerika ichijōsha* [Commodore Perry's Expedition to Hakodate...] (Hakodate, Japan, 1953), pages 26–27; English text, pages 16–17.

[47]*SI-AR 1858,* page 53.

[48]Morison, *Old Bruin,* page 424.

[49]In addition to the description in the text, see *Bakumatsu gaikoku ...,* volume 8, pages 532–556, which includes a list, submitted by Ido Tsushima-no-kami to senior councilors of the *Bakufu,* of the articles prepared in April 1854 to be given as additional gifts to the American expedition party and the bazaars to be held for them at Shimoda.

[50]Ibid., volume 6, pages 197–202, for the memorandum and the American want list dated 24 May 1854, submitted by the reception commissioners to senior members of the *shōgun*'s council, *Shimoda machi bugyō shoruisho-shū gaikoku jiken sho* [Shimoda (city) Magistrate Records Relating to Foreign Affairs] and Appendix V for the English translation of the list.

[51]For a list of the articles for sale reported to be coarse or inferior, see Fusui Mori, editor, *Kurofune dansō* [Collected Essays on (the coming of) Black Ships] (Shimoda, Japan, 1942), page 139.

[52]*Williams Journal,* page 27. Hora, *Peri Nihon,* page 59, gives the Japanese translation of Williams' description of the gifts as *"mikake taoshi no shina-jina"* (showy but worthless articles). Cf. note number 42 for the assorted articles Perry purchased at Naha.

[53]The *rōjū* were councilors to the Shōgun and officials of the Edo Bakufu. The *rōjū* were elected from among the hereditary daimyō (lords).

[54]Ernest Mason Satow, *Japan 1853–1864,* or *Genji yume monogatari,* (Tokyo, 1905), page 4 [The Japanese translation of *Kaikoku shidan* (History of the Opening of Japan), by Baba Bun'ei].

[55]Perry's letter of 5 September 1853, Maco, to the President of the United States, deposited in the Huntington Library (MS).

[56]*Perry Journal,* pages 101–102.

[57]*Hawks Narrative,* page 312.

[58]Bayard Taylor, *A Visit to India, China, and Japan in the Year 1853* (New York, 1859), page 438. Taylor was a civilian who joined the expedition party at Hong Kong.

[59]*Perry Journal,* page 190.

[60]*Preble Diary,* pages 144–146, for his 24 March 1854 entry.

[61]*Perry Journal,* page 190.

[62]*Preble Diary,* page 146.

[63]Ibid., page 150.

[64]Allan B. Cole, editor, *With Perry in Japan: The Diary of Edward Yorke McCauley, Acting Master's Mate in Powhatan* (Princeton, 1942), page 99.

[65]*Williams Journal,* page 145.

[66]Ibid.

[67]Shio Sakanishi, editor, *A Private Journal of John Glendy Sproston, U.S.N.* (Tokyo, 1940), page 11. Hereafter, this will be referred to as *Sproston Journal.*

[68]*Morrow Journal,* pages 145–146.

[69]Griffis, *Matthew Calbraith Perry,* page 369.

[70]Robert Tomes, *The Americans in Japan: An Abridgement of the Government Narrative of the U.S. Expedition to Japan, under Commodore Perry* (1857), page 232.

[71]Statler, *Black Ship Scroll,* page 12.

[72]Morison, *Old Bruin,* page 424. The exchange rate imposed on the Americans in 1854 was 1 *ryō* to approximately \$4.30; it was 1 *ryō* to approximately \$1.35 for the Dutch at Nagasaki. See Hora, *Peri Nihon,* page 347.

[73]For the Shimoda gift list, see the document, an excerpt from "Kokui ōsetsu-roku" [The Reception Commissioners' Records Relating to the Black (ship) Barbarians (Americans)], in *Bakumatsu gaikoku ...,* 1914, volume 6, pages 310–313 (cf. Appendix III).

[74]"Kokui ōsetsu-roku," in *Bakumatsu gaikoku ...,* supplement volume 1, page 573. *Morrow Journal,* page 193.

[75]*Hawks Narrative,* page 556.

[76]*Williams Journal,* page 205. The additional American gifts were four howitzers from the *Powhatan* and *Mississippi.* These were given to Ido and Izawa. The two cannons subsequently were presented to the shogunal government. See *Morrow Journal,* page 192.

[77]Hora, *Peri Nihon,* page 341. For his assessment of the Shimoda presents see Tomio Hora "Kaikoku to Shimoda" [The Opening of Japan and Shimoda]. In *Izu Shimoda* (Tokyo, 1962), page 695.

[78]*Williams Journal,* page 216.

[79]*Williams Journal,* page 245. *Hawks Narrative,* page 571, mentions only the temple bell; so does Speiden, see his entry for 12 July 1854, Naha, Speiden Journal. The episode goes unmentioned in the *Perry Journal.*

[80]A *han,* literally hedge or palisade, was a fief or territory governed by a *daimyō.*

[81]See Hora, *Peri Nihon,* pages 466–486, for the Japanese document entitled "Peri kantai Okinawa raikō kankei Satsuma han Naha zaiban bugyō todokesho" [The Reports Relative to Perry Squadron's Okinawa Visits by the Naha *bugyō* Appointed by Satsuma *han*]. For the list, ibid., 484–485. Installed in a specially constructed belfry, the bell stood at the entrance to Bancroft Hall at the U.S. Naval Academy until 22 July 1987 when the bell was returned to Japan. It is now housed in the Okinawa Prefectural Museum at Naha. Sources such as *Okinawa bunka-shi jiten* [Dictionary of Okinawan Cultural History] (Tokyo, 1977), page 506; George H. Kerr, *Okinawa: The History of an Island People* (Vermont and Tokyo, 1965), page 337; and the records of the U.S. Naval Academy, identify the bell as coming from the Gokoku-ji temple. Other sources, such as Ryōhei Tsuboi, *Nihon no bonshō* [Japanese Buddhist Temple Bells] (Tokyo, 1970), pages 234–235, 436; and Seikō Hokama, Ryūkyū no bonshō ni tsute, in *Bunkazai yōran* [A Survey of the (Ryūkyūan) Cultural Properties] (Naha, 1961), pages 97–98, consider it to be a bell from the Daian zen-ji. The apparent confusion stems from the fact that the Daian zen-ji, for which the bell was cast and hung originally, is no longer extant, and the bell subsequently was moved to the Gokoku-ji some time following the construction of Gokoku-ji in 1713. See Seimo Nakayama, editor, *Ryūkyū-shi jiten* [An Historical Dictionary of the Ryūkyūs] (Naha, 1969), pages 484–486; also Okinawa Taimususha, editor, *Okinawa daihyakka jiten* [Encyclopaedia of Okinawa] (Naha, 1983), pages 640–641. The bell's dimensions are given by Tsuboi, page 235, and Hokama, page 98, as: height 76.2 cm; diameter 62.0 cm; weight approximately 100 kg. Mrs. Perry presented the bell to the U.S. Naval Academy in 1859, after the Commodore's death, in accordance with her husband's wishes.

[82]Regarding the stone from Shimoda, see Yoshio Mori, *Peri to Shimoda kaikō* (Shimoda, 1969), page 141, which illustrates the Japanese inscription; see also Speiden's entry for 29 July 1854, Speiden Journal.

[83]For a description of the White House showing, see Masao Miyoshi, *As We Saw Them: The First Japanese Embassy to the United States (1860)* (Berkeley, California, 1979), page 132. There is a probability that some of the Perry items may have been on public view prior to their transfer to the Smithsonian in 1858. The Maryland Institute for the Promotion of Mechanic Arts proposed to include "Japan Curiosities" in their annual exhibition to be held on 2 October 1855. The Commissioner of the Patent Office gave his approbation. See the 2 September 1855 letter of Johan Vansard, President of the Maryland Institute to S.T. Shugert, Commissioner of the Patent Office. The letter is in the Huntington Library (MS).

[84]The June 2nd Japanese visit to the Smithsonian was reported in an article headed "Movements of the Japanese," in the *New York Herald,* 4 June 1860. See Library of Congress newspaper collection, microfilm reel number 2128. A Japanese translation of the *NYH* article is in Kanai, *Man'en gannen ...,* pages 29–30. See also Varden Papers, diary entry for 2 June 1860.

[85]The 1968 Smithsonian Institution exhibition catalog entitled "The Japan Expedition 1852–1855 of Commodore Matthew Calbraith Perry" lists these items under the heading, "Japanese gifts." Some items so listed have since been identified either as non-Perry materials or purchased articles.

[86]See the ethnology collection card catalog file and loan record in the Department of Anthropology Processing Laboratory. See also the Naval Historical Foundation Registrar's files located in Navy Historical Center, Navy Yard, Washington, D.C.

[87]Eugenie M. Guilmette letter of 22 July 1976 to Philip K. Lundberg, in the National Museum of American History Registrar's Office, accession number 1977.0186.

[88]The Thomas C. Dudley Japan Expedition Journal is in the collections of the William L. Clements Library, University of Michigan.

Catalog

Entries uniformly begin with the closest equivalent English term, then the native Japanese term, including variants, if any. Collection identification, e.g., USNM Ethnology collection, NMAH Division of Naval History (now renamed the Division of Armed Forces), Dudley collection, etc., and catalog number are given next, followed by the object's dimensions in centimeters (D = diameter, H = height, L = length, T = thickness, W = width).

The caption contents are intended to present the following information, generally in this order: (1) description of physical form, component materials, methods of construction, and decoration; (2) uses of the object, including identification of users, functions, and manner and condition of use; (3) elaboration of 1 and 2 in terms of relevant traditions, symbolism, historical origins and development, and typicality, plus supporting references to identical or similar specimens in other museum or private collections; (4) identification and interpretation of inscriptions, seals, and other marks; (5) variant and often erroneous identifications, which may be indicative of certain misperceptions of the times, in extant Smithsonian records (e.g., the original 1859 Smithsonian Anthropology catalog book number 1, the 1953 accession file number 199043, and the current Ethnology collection [card] catalog), along with comparative entries in various published and unpublished sources; (6) name, location, and date of exhibition, if the object was shown in the past or is presently on display; and (7) donor's or purchaser's name, location, and date, if established.

Japanese names are given following the native practice of giving surname first, before the given name. The modified Hepburn transliteration system is used for renderings of Japanese terms as well as personal and place names.

LIST OF ABBREVIATIONS

The following abbreviations identify various lists of Japanese presents; the list of Japanese objects wanted by members of the American expedition party; lists of merchandise prepared to give as additional gifts, for sale at bazaars, and those items actually purchased; select private and museum collection and exhibition catalogs of premodern Japanese artifacts; Smithsonian museums and administrative divisions; accession and catalog records; and dictionaries and technical and other special reference works cited. See "Literature Cited" for fuller descriptions.

AWL	American Want List [containing various Japanese articles desired by the Americans, submitted by the Reception Commissioners to the Senior Council] in *Bakumatsu gaikoku kankei monjo*, volume 6 [cf. Appendix V]. [In the "Literature Cited" under Tokyo University Histographical Institute.]
BGKM	*Bakumatsu gaikoku kankei monjo* [Official Documents Relating to Foreign Relations in the Late Edo Period]. [In the "Literature Cited" under Tokyo University Historiographical Institute.]
BT	*Bijutsu techō* [Handbook of (Japanese) Art]. [In the "Literature Cited" under Tokyo bijutsu kurabu seinenkai, editor.]
CCJWA	*Descriptive Catalogue of General Horace Capron's Collection of Specimens of Antique Japanese Works of Art Temporarily Deposited in the U.S. National Museum* [collection catalog]. [In the "Literature Cited" under Smithsonian Institution.]
ECC	Ethnology Collection [Card] Catalog [Located in the Department of Anthropology, National Museum of Natural History, Smithsonian Institution.]
HL	Hora Tomio's list of Japanese presents in *Peri Nihon ensei zuikō-ki* [Japanese translation of *A Journal of the Perry Expedition to Japan*, by S. Wells Williams].
HNL	Hawks' Narrative list [of Japanese presents] in *Narrative of the Expedition of an American Squadron to the China Sea and Japan...* by Francis L. Hawks.
JI	Japanese Interiors. [In the "Literature Cited" under Gakuyō shobō Editorial Board.]
KORL	"Kokui ōsetsu roku" (The Reception Commissioners' Records Relating to the Black [Ship] Barbarians [Americans]) list [of Japanese presents] in *BGKM*, volume 5.
ML	Morrow list [of articles purchased at Hakodate and Shimoda] in *A Scientist with Perry in Japan: The Journal of Dr. James Morrow*, edited by Allan B. Cole.
NGL	"Nyoze gamon" (As the Way I Heard) list [of Japanese presents] in *BGKM*, volume 4.
NKDJ	*Nihon kokugo daijiten* (Encyclopaedia of Japanese Language). [In the "Literature Cited" under Nihon daijiten kankōkai, editor.]
NMAH	Smithsonian Institution, National Museum of American History.
NMAH-DAF	Smithsonian Institution, National Museum of American History, Division of Armed Forces.
NMAH-DT	Smithsonian Institution, National Museum of American History, Division of Textiles.

NMNH	Smithsonian Institution, National Museum of Natural History.
NMNH-NAA	Smithsonian Institution, National Museum of Natural History, National Anthropological Archives.
OSL	"Okinawa-ken shiryō" list [Historical documents relating to Okinawa Prefecture]. [In the "Literature Cited" under Okinawa-ken Okinawa shiryō henshūsho, editor.]
PJL	Perry Journal list [of Japanese presents] in *The Japan Expedition 1852–1854; the Personal Journal of Commodore Matthew C. Perry,* edited by Rodger Pineau.
SGL	Shimoda gift list [containing additional Japanese gifts presented at Shimoda] in *BGKM,* volume 6.
SML	"Shimoda machi-bugyō" (city magistrate) list [of the articles assembled as additional gifts promised and also items to be sold at the bazaars held for the Americans May–June 1854 at Shimoda] in *BGKM,* volume 8.

UD	*Ueda's daijiten: A Japanese Dictionary of Chinese Characters and Compounds.* [In the "Literature Cited" under Harvard University.]
USKH	*Ukiyo-e no sekai-teki kyoshō Hiroshige ten* (An Exhibition of Hiroshige's Masterpieces) [exhibition catalog].
USNM	Collections of the former United States National Museum, now in the National Museum of Natural History, Smithsonian Institution.
1859-ACB	1859 Smithsonian Institution Anthropology catalog, book number 1.
1953-AL	1953 Smithsonian Institution Accession list (NMNH, Office of the Registrar, accession file 199043).
1968-SIJE	1968 Smithsonian Institution Japan Expedition exhibit list in *The Japan Expedition 1852–1855 of Commodore Matthew Calbraith Perry* [exhibition catalog]. [In the "Literature Cited" under Smithsonian Institution.]

Lacquerware

1 Lacquered covered bowl (*suimonowan* 吸物椀)
USNM ECC 6
H: 8.4 cm, D: 11.5 cm

Description: Black lacquer, conical, wooden soup bowl with cover and foot rim.

Characteristics: A gold and silver thistle design of *keshifun makie* 消粉蒔絵 (sprinkled or strewn gold or silver dust; for various other types of *makie* decorations and standard terms, see Komatsu, 1975:86) decorates the cover and one side of the bowl. The bowl interior is in red, whereas the bowl and cover rims are in gold.

Remarks: This bowl probably was purchased at Shimoda. An entry for "*akikusa no moyō suimonowan rokujūnin-mae*" 秋草之模様吸物椀六拾人前 (sixty lacquered soup bowls decorated with autumn grass design) is recorded in the SML (see *BGKM,* 1916, volume 8, page 547, for entry) in response to the AWL (cf. Appendix V). The bowl was exhibited at the Japan Society, New York City, in 1969 and also was included in the National Portrait Gallery's exhibit, "Mission to Japan," in Washington, D.C., in 1978.

Additional Specimens: ECC 7, cover missing; ECC 13, cover missing; ECC 14, bowl missing (2 complete sets remaining). All have dimensions identical to the illustrated specimen.

2 Lacquered covered bowl (*suimonowan*)
USNM ECC 180
H: 5.5 cm, D: 10.8 cm

Description: Vermilion lacquer soup bowl with cover and foot rim.

Characteristics: The interior and exterior surfaces of the bowl and the bowl cover are in vermilion with no ornamentation.

Remarks: The bowl was not included in any of the official lists of Japanese presents. Most likely it was part of the 50 lacquer cups [bowls] presented to Perry at Edo Bay by Kayama Eizaemon (Assistant Magistrate of Uraga) on 16 July 1853 (Williams, 1910:67–68), which were sent subsequently to the White House (Perry letter of 5 September 1853, Macao, to the President of the United States).

Additional Specimens: Eighteen sets (ECC 137–148, 177–182), including two incomplete sets: ECC 148, bowl missing; ECC 178, cover missing.

USNM ECC 6

USNM ECC 180

USNM ECC 8

3 Lacquered covered bowl (*suimonowan*)
USNM ECC 8
H: 9.8 cm, D: 11.5 cm

Description: Dark olive green lacquer, conical bowl with cover and foot rim.

Characteristics: A design of stylized maple leaves in red and gold *makie* decorates the cover and one side of the bowl. The interior surface is red, whereas the bowl and cover rims are in gold.

Remarks: It probably was purchased at Shimoda sometime during May–June 1854 (cf. entry 1 for references). The bowl was exhibited at the Japan Society, New York City, in 1969 and also at the National Portrait Gallery, Washington, D.C., in 1978.

Additional Specimens: ECC 9, bowl only; ECC 11, bowl with cover; ECC 12 bowl only; all with dimensions similar to those of ECC 8.

4 Lacquered bowl (*suimonowan*)
USNM ECC 10 (not illustrated)
H: 5 cm, D: 11.8 cm

Description: Dark red lacquer, conical, gold rimmed bowl with foot rim and cover missing.

Characteristics: Scattered gold dots decorate one side of the bowl.

Remarks: This bowl definitely was not part of the 50 red lacquered covered bowls received in 1853 (cf. entry 2); furthermore, it is unlikely to have been part of an official gift. No reference to it has been found in the various lists.

NMAH-DAF Dudley 59873-N-0076–77
Above, lacquered base and view of
overturned bowl.
Right, lacquered covered bowl on stand,
side view.

5 Lacquered covered bowl with stand (*suimonowan*)
NMAH-DAF Dudley 59873-N-0076-77
H: 8.4 cm, D: 11.5 cm

Description: Conical wooden soup bowl in black lacquer,
with cover, foot rim, and stand.

Characteristics: The footed and slightly grooved stand has
a recessed (D: 12.7 cm) center into which the bowl's foot rim
fits. A rose-colored *botan* 牡丹 (peony) in gold *makie* decorates
the exterior cover, and an outline of leaves in gold is on one
sector of the bowl's exterior. The interior surface is in ochre,
whereas the bowl and cover rims are in gold.

Remarks: This probably was purchased at one of the
several bazaars held in Shimoda in 1854. "*Kiku makie
suimonowan rokujū-nin mae*" 菊蒔絵吸物椀六拾人前
(sixty sets of soup bowls with floral *makie* decoration) were
included in the items prepared for the bazaars to be held in
Shimoda for the Americans (*BGKM,* 1916, volume 8, page
540). The bowl, a gift of E.M. Guilmette, a descendant of the
collector, was received in 1977.

USNM ECC 158

6 Lacquered shallow bowl (*nurizarawan* 塗皿椀)
USNM ECC 158
H: 6.2 cm, D: 18 cm

Description: Shallow, wooden, dark red lacquered bowl with low foot rim, used for serving food.

Characteristics: The interior is decorated with gold *makie* design of auspicious symbols. Depicted are three figures of long-tailed *minogame* 蓑亀 (lit. straw-raincoat tortoise), a longevity symbol that is derived from the legend of the messenger from the Sea God, whose tail is said to grow when it is 500 years old (Dower, 1971:100; Boger, 1964:24; Newman and Ryerson, 1964:56, for legend and symbolism). The *minogame* rest onshore above the waves, which are symbolic of power and resilience (Dower, 1971:44), among clusters of pine needles. Common symbolic attributes for pine are longevity, morality, and constancy (Casal, 1961, glossary 25). The bowl rim is in gold.

Remarks: There is an entry for "*nurizarawan*" in the AWL (cf. Appendix V), and the bowl was described as one of three "wooden highly ornamented red bowls" in the 1953-AL (cf. Appendix VI). Black-and-white photographs of this bowl previously were published by Lancaster (1963:18) as an illustration of Japanese presents to Perry. The caption described it as a "bowl in red and gold lacquer."

Additional Specimens: ECC 156, H: 4.8 cm, D: 14.9 cm; ECC 157, H: 5.5 cm, D: 16.3 cm. These two bowls and ECC 158 nest together to form a set.

7 Covered lacquerware bowl (*shiruwan* 汁椀)
USNM ECC 15 (bowl) and ECC 17 (cover) (not illustrated)
H: 5.5 cm, D: 10 cm

Description: Dull black lacquered bowl slightly tapered toward the foot and cover, with foot rim in dull black lacquer, used for serving soup or food prepared in broth.

Characteristics: A *shiruwan* (lit. soup bowl; also bowl used for serving various nondry dishes) is somewhat smaller in size but less shallow than the common *suimonowan* (soup bowl) (see Janata, 1965, entries 372e, 373, for similar specimens; *NKDJ,* 1976, volume 11, page 81, for varied uses). The finish is in the style of *tsuya-keshi* 艶消し (sheen-extinguished) and *hakeme-nuri* 刷け目塗 (lacquer paint that shows traces of the brush strokes) (Casal, 1961:14–15, for the techniques used to produce this particular type of lacquered finish).

Remarks: This bowl possibly was from Hayashi Daigaku-no-kashira. According to a PJL entry, there was "1 box of 3 lacquered cups"; and an HNL entry reads: "1 box, set of 3,

USNM ECC 16

lacquered goblets." Possibly it was a purchased item because the AWL includes *zenwan* 膳椀 (tableware, food serving bowls) (*BGKM,* 1914, volume 6, page 201). The 1859-ACB identifies it as a wooden black bowl. It was exhibited at the Japan Society, New York City, in 1969.

Additional Specimens: Two additional bowls each without a cover, both with dimensions of H: 7 cm, D: 10.5 cm. One bowl has duplicate number ECC 15, the other has duplicate number ECC 17.

8 Covered lacquerware bowl (*shiruwan*)
USNM ECC 16
H: 7.2 cm, D: 10.7 cm

Description: Lacquered wooden bowl and cover, both with foot rims.

Characteristics: The rust-colored finish is produced by combining the *sabiji* 錆地 (rust-ground) and *hakeme-nuri* methods. The bowl's size is somewhat smaller but taller than the common *suimonowan* (soup bowl) (for descriptions and uses see *NKDJ,* 1976, volume 11, page 81; Janata, 1965, entries 372e, 373).

Remarks: This bowl may have been received from Hayashi Daigaku-no-kashira, if it corresponds to a PJL entry for "1 box of 3 lacquered cups" and an HNL entry for "1 box, set of 3, lacquered goblets." The AWL also includes *zenwan* for the bazaars to be held in Shimoda (*BGKM,* 1914, volume 6, page 201). The bowl was exhibited at the Japan Society, New York City, in 1969.

Additional Specimens: ECC 19, bowl with cover missing; H: 7.5 cm, D: 10.8 cm.

USNM ECC 71 (gold lacquered box with lid on)

9 Lacquered stationery box (*ryōshi-bako* 料紙箱)
USNM ECC 71
L: 40.5 cm, W: 33 cm, H: 17 cm

Description: Black, rectangular, covered lacquer box with shallow interior tray, used for storing paper, brushes, inkstones, and other writing paraphernalia.

Characteristics: The box cover ornamentation is in the traditionally auspicious *shōchikubai* 松竹梅 (pine, bamboo, and plum) design of *makie* decoration in relief against the *nashiji* 梨地 (lit. golden pear-like color finish; gold flecked surface) lacquer finish. The *nashiji* exterior finish is obtained by sprinkling gold flakes, made from compressed coarse gold fillings, onto the surface and applying a final coating of lacquer. Additional decoration includes such other equally auspicious symbols as clouds and waves in burnished gold. The interior surface is finished in black lacquer. Boxes of this size and construction generally are known simply as *ryōshi-bako* (stationery box) (Young, 1973:112, 206, for the term and similar specimens).

Remarks: This stationery box was presented as a gift to the President of the United States from the *Bakufu* (the military government under the shōgun; also known as the Shogunate Government, 1603–1868) at Kanagawa in March 1854. An entry for "*nashiji makie shōchikubai ryōshi suzuri-bako*" 梨地蒔絵松竹梅料紙硯箱 appears in the NGL (*BGKM*, 1912, volume 4, page 556), and "*Ryōshi suzuri-bako, shōchikubai taka-makie*" is recorded in the SML (*BGKM*, 1916, volume 8, page 546).

USNM ECC 71 (detailed view of front of box)

USNM ECC 71 (three-quarter view of front and side of box, lid removed)

USNM ECC 71 (view of underside of box lid)

USNM ECC 72 (inside view of lacquered inkstone box)

10 Lacquered inkstone box (*suzuri-bako*)
USNM ECC 72
L: 24.5 cm, W: 20.5 cm, H: 4.5 cm

Description: Square covered lacquered box with *nashiji* finish.

Characteristics: The interior surface of the box cover is decorated with figures of *minogame,* a legendary, long-tailed tortoise (cf. entry 6 for symbolism), in *makie* relief design. Encased in the box are a rectangular black inkstone, a round metal *mizu-ire* 水入れ (water-dropper) decorated with a carved pine tree design, a writing brush, and a gimlet with a small book of note paper. The lower interior surface of the inkstone box has additional floral *makie* ornamentation in a dandelion design. An inkstone box also is referred to as a writing box, and it usually is placed on a scholar's desk.

Remarks: This *suzuri-bako* probably was received from Ido Tsushima-no-kami and Izawa Mimasaka-no-kami at Shimoda (*BGKM,* 1914, volume 6, page 311 for entry) in response to a want-listed item included in the AWL (cf. Appendix V). There is another entry for *suzuri-bako* in the KORL (*BGKM,* 1914, volume 5, page 310), in which case this inkstone box was included in the Reception Committee's official list of Japanese gifts. The box was included in the Cooper-Hewitt Museum of Decorative Arts and Design's exhibit, "Writing and Reading," New York City, during 15 September 1981–3 January 1982.

USNM ECC 72 (detail of top of lid)

USNM ECC 152

11   Lacquered waiter (*ken'gai; suzuri-buta* 硯蓋)
USNM ECC 152(a,b)
L: 24 cm, W: 22.5 cm, H: 2.5 cm; L: 23 cm, W: 21 cm,
H: 2.5 cm

Description: Two sets (with identical dimensions) of nested square trays, each set with two trays having rounded corners, lacquered black exteriors, and lacquered red interiors.

Characteristics: Trays such as these are used for serving fruit or sweets (pers. comm. Hauge, letter, 23 July 1992), and for presenting flowers (*NKDJ,* 1969, volume 11, page 431). *Ken'gai* or *suzuri-buta* literally means the cover of an inkstone box, but its usage is equivalent to that of a tray or waiter.

Remarks: The HNL (cf. Appendix I) enters them as "1 set [of] waiters" for the "Government of the United States of America, from the Emperor," and also as "2 boxes lacquered waiters, 4 in all" from Ido, 2nd Commissioner. But the PJL (cf. Appendix II) enters them as "1 set of two lacquered trays." Assuming that one set normally consists of two trays, these two sets, "4 in all," may be the ones given by Ido. They initially were translated as "*urushinuri-kyūjibon*" 漆塗給仕盆 (lacquered waiters), but this was corrected to read "*ken'gai* or *suzuri-buta*" in the HL (Hora, 1970:242). They were listed as "black working box" in the 1953-AL. One set was exhibited at the Japan Society, New York City, in 1969.

USNM ECC 20

12 Lidded lacquerware box (*meshi-bako* 飯箱 ; *bentō* 弁当)
USNM ECC 20
L: 23 cm, W: 24.3 cm, H: 6.8 cm

Description: Square wooden black lacquered *meshi-bako* (food box) or *bentō* (lunch box), locally called by Okinawans "*hatssun-jūbako*" 八寸重箱 (8 *ssun* [1 *ssun* = 3.3 cm], ~24 cm × ~24 cm size tiered food box) even when not tiered (pers. comm. Gibo, conversation, 16 January 1990).

Characteristics: The lid border is ornamented with a lacquered painting of *shōchikubai* motif in red. An additional floral design of red chrysanthemum blossom decorates the center of the lid and the four sides of the box. The interior is finished with red lacquer, whereas the bottom of the box is covered with clear lacquer, revealing the dark, wood surface.

Remarks: This probably is one of the assorted lacquerwares (cf. Appendixes IIIB, IIID) that was received at Naha (Hora, 1970:59; also Williams, 1910:27, for his 8 June 1853 journal entry). Both the 1859-ACB and 1953-AL identify it as "Loo Choo wooden work box."

USNM ECC 21

13   Lidded lacquerware box (*meshi-bako; bentō*)
USNM ECC 21
L: 20 cm, W: 21.5 cm, H: 6.5 cm

Description: Shallow, square, wooden box with lid.
Characteristics: Although both the interior and exterior of the box are vermilion, the bottom is in black lacquer. This style of box is used as a lunch box for cold dishes or sweets, or for delivering such articles to friends and relatives. Faint traces of the imprint: "Chow Chow Box Loo Choo" is apparent on the lid.

Remarks: This box was received at Naha and was recorded in Williams' journal as "*meshibako*" (lit. rice box) (Hora, 1970:484), and as "*bentō*" (lunch box) (Hora, 1970:470). It also is known as "*rokssun-jūbako*" 六寸重箱 (6 *ssun*, ~20 cm × ~20 cm size tiered food box) (pers. comm. Gibo, conversation, 16 January 1990; cf. entry 12 for usage of the term). It probably was included in an "assortment of lacquerwares" received (cf. Appendixes IIIB, IIID) and was so identified by Williams (1910:27, for his 8 June 1853 journal entry).

14 Lacquered boxes (*kobako* 小箱 ; *tebako* 手箱)
USNM ECC 154, 155
L: 14 cm, W: 14 cm, H: 8.7 cm

Description: Small, square, wooden, covered box with low foot rim in black lacquer finish with *raden* 螺鈿 *aogai* (blue shell) and nacre inlay decoration (Casal, 1961:25; Komatsu, 1975:86, for the *raden* method of ornamentation) combined with the *fuse saishiki* 伏彩色 (application of pigments over shell inlays) method of embellishment (pers. comm. Komatsu, conversation, January 1989).

Characteristics: Lacquered boxes such as these are popularly known as a *tebako* (handy box), *kobako* (small box), or a cosmetic box. They are used to store small, precious objects or small articles for everyday use. The tops of the covers are ornamented with a floral design of magnolia (ECC 154) and camellia (ECC 155) blossoms in shaded pink, with branches and leaves in iridescent lavender and blue-green. The four sides of each box have painted nacre inlays of plum blossoms and petals. According to legend (local legend of Aomori Prefecture), the *mokuran* 木蘭 or magnolia is a symbol of spring and of feminine sweetness and beauty, whereas the camellia or *tsubaki* 椿 symbolizes success in love (Joya, 1958:235, for the legendary *tsubaki yama* 椿山 (camellia mountain) in Aomori).

Remarks: Komatsu Taishū (pers. comm., conversation, January 1989) identified these as Nagasaki-*mono* 長崎物 , the typical souvenir lacquerware produced in Nagasaki for export. They probably were received from Ido at Shimoda in June 1854, and they are listed in the KORL as "*raden-bako*" (cf. Appendix III). ECC 155 was included in the "Men Who Made the Navy" exhibit at the Truxtun Decatur Naval Museum, Washington, D.C., in 1975–1976, and later in the exhibit "Mission to Japan" at the National Portrait Gallery, Smithsonian Institution, in 1978.

Additional Specimens: ECC 153, with a floral design of magnolia on the cover top, similar to that of ECC 154.

USNM ECC 154

USNM ECC 155

USNM ECC 23, 162

15 Lacquerware picnic box (*bentō-bako* 弁当箱 ; *sagejū-bako* 下重箱)
USNM ECC 23, 162
L: 14 cm, W: 22.5 cm, H: 21.5 cm

Description: Sagejū style (layered containers fitted into a box with carrying handle) rectangular wooden (oak, pers. comm. Tanabe, conversation, June 1979) box with clear lacquer finish.

Characteristics: The box has a sliding front panel, copper fittings on the front exterior corners, and two round escutcheons in front and back of the loop handle on the box top. Fitted inside are five boxes (two are lidded) of various sizes in red lacquer, a box-shaped pewter wine bottle (Boger, 1964:94, for Japanese use of pewter) with a spout and covered opening at the top, and a small conical cup (3 cm in diameter). All five box exterior bottoms are in black lacquer (for varied styles of construction, ornamentation, uses, and the popularity of the *sagejū* style picnic box during the Edo period, see Young, 1977: 125–126; also Okamura, 1946, fig. 80, a "*shunuri bentō-bako*" (*sagejū* style lunch box in vermilion lacquer) for an Okinawan type).

Remarks: During the 19th century, Westerners often referred to this type of picnic box as a "tea chest," and this piece is so identified in the 1859-ACB and 1953-AL. It is not included in the PJL nor in the HNL. It was received from Hayashi if it is the item identified as "chow-chow box" (Hora, 1970:242, for HL; cf. Appendixes I, II). One small lidded box top is numbered 162 in error.

USNM ECC 163

16 Lacquered picnic box (*bentō-bako; sagejū-bako*)
USNM ECC 163
L: 14 cm, W: 24 cm, H: 21.3 cm

Description: *Sagejū* style rectangular wooden (oak, pers. comm. Tanabe, conversation, June 1979) box with clear lacquer finish.

Characteristics: The picnic box has a sliding front panel and a looped copper handle at the top. In front and back of the handle two round copper escutcheons are attached. Four covered bowls are fitted inside; two cylindrical vessels on the lower shelf and two smaller, somewhat globular, vessels on the upper shelf. The bowl exteriors are decorated with an ochre finish of *suki-urushi* 透漆 *mokume-nuri* 木目漆 (tinted clear

lacquer finish to show the wood grain), and the interiors are covered with red lacquer (Casal, 1961:14–15, especially for the type of lacquer finish). This type of finish that shows the wood grain also is known as *shunkei-nuri* 春慶塗 , the technique developed during the Muromachi period (1392–1569) by lacquer artist Shunkei (pers. comm. Komatsu, conversation, June 1979). Note that this type of *sagejū* is used not only for outings but for the social and commercial delivery of prepared foods (*NKDJ,* 1976, volume 8, page 696).

Remarks: This picnic box is not included in any published or unpublished lists of Japanese presents. It was received from Hayashi if it is the item referred to as "chow-chow box" (Hora, 1970:242, for HL; Appendixes I, II).

Textiles and Paper

17 Silk (*kempu* 絹布 ; *kinu* 絹)
NMAH-DT E4097, E4099 (original nos. unknown)
W: 35.5–41.0 cm, L: 5 rolls (1 roll = ~2¹/₂ yards)

Description: Kohaku hira-ori 琥珀平織 (evenly balanced, plain weave silk) taffeta with multicolored *yoko-jima* 横縞 (horizontal stripes) design.

Characteristics: Yoko-jima designs are woven with ikat dyed weft (pers. comm. Fiske, letter, 24 October 1979). E4097 (41.0 cm wide) has horizontal stripes in blue, tan, brown, red, and yellow; E4099 (35.5 cm wide) has horizontal stripes in blue, red, tan, and grey. The *kohaku-ori* 琥珀織 (lit. textile with smooth-as-amber texture) (*NKDJ,* 1976, volume 4, page 223, for the term) silk taffeta was introduced to Japan in the 16th century by immigrant Chinese weavers in Sakai 堺 (then a major port and center of commerce; now a suburb of modern Osaka), who contributed greatly to the development of Japanese weaving techniques (Shively, 1968:250). Stripes as woven design were said to have been known to the Japanese first as *tōzan* 唐桟 (Chinese wood lattice work) and later as *shima* 島 (lit. island; homonym of *shima* 縞, stripes and checks), which is derived from the term for *shima-mono* 島物 (articles of south-sea island origin). By the late 17th century and early 18th century, stripes were the most popular textile pattern (see Hauge and Hauge, 1978:26, for the history of stripes, especially as woven designs in cotton). Because Tokugawa law prohibited the possession of silk by commoners, silk fabrics were worn exclusively by persons of high station. Rich silk costumes were in heavy demand with actors in the aristocratic *nō* 能 drama; the *dandara-jima* 段段縞 (multicolored stripes) design was reserved for a type of *nō* silken costume called *noshime* 熨斗目 (plain, short- or small-sleeved garment), which was worn by actors playing the roles of old men, Buddhist priests, common people, low-ranking samurai, and low-born women of mature years (for types of *nō*

costumes and associated textile designs, and for illustrations of *noshime* in variegated colored, horizontal stripes, see Noma, 1974:58–65, 150). Only after 1714 were *kabuki* actors allowed to use silk costumes (Shively, 1968:255), and the Tokugawa shogunate granted special permission in 1787 for those of samurai status to wear silken garments of striped design. Even the multicolored striped pattern that included red, a color traditionally associated with femininity, became popular among men (Noma, 1974:132–133). Following the Meiji restoration (1868), silk became available for commoners' apparel, and silk taffeta was widely used for various types of clothing and as suitable fabrics for umbrellas and parasols (see *UD,* 1942:1503, for various usages). Twenty-four or 25 *tan* 反 (approximately 12 yards per *tan*) were presented to the Americans by *bakufu* councillors at Kanagawa in March 1854 (cf. Appendixes I, II). The offering of textiles in gift-giving is an important aspect of Japanese tradition (pers. comm. Hauge, letter, 23 July 1992), which has ceremonial significance "as an expression of respect" (Miyoshi, 1979:50).

Remarks: These five rolls of silk have been variously identified as "striped-figured silk (taffeta)" (HNL; PJL), "*gunnai-jima kaiki*" 柳条峡絹 (lit. silk decorated with thin, willow branch-like lines) (KORL in *BGKM,* 1914, volume 5, pages 313–314; NGL in *BGKM,* 1912, volume 4, pages 560–561), "*gunnai-jima kaiki*" 郡内縞甲斐絹 (stripe-patterned silk from the Kai 甲斐 district (modern Yamanshi prefecture) (*NKDJ,* 1976, volume 7, page 67)), and "*kohaku-ori*" (HL in Hora, 1970:242). They were entered as "assorted silk pieces" in the 1859-ABC and USNM-ECC. E4099 has been renumbered as T1887? by the Division of Textiles, Smithsonian Institution.

Additional Specimens: E4059 (41 cm wide) has horizontal stripes in pink, red, blue, and tan; E4098 (35.5 cm wide) has two tones of blue and grey horizontal stripes; and E4100 (36 cm wide) has horizontal stripes in blue, red, brown, and tan.

NMAH-DT E4097

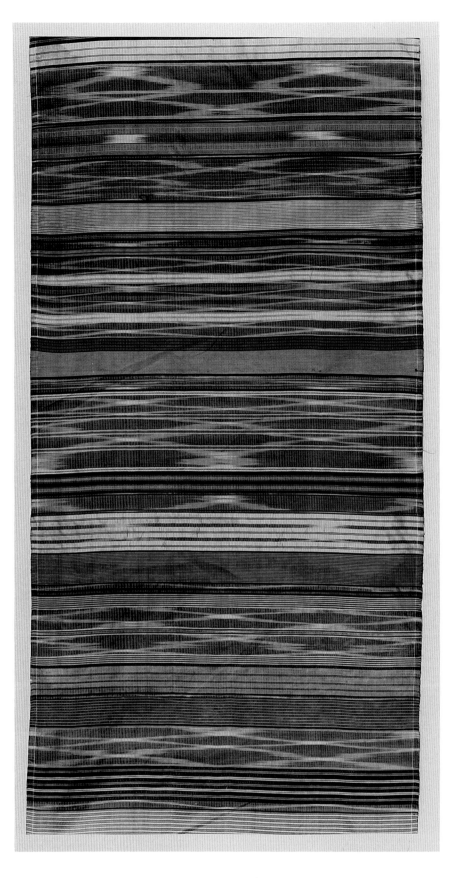

NMAH-DT E4099

NMAH-DT E4060

18 Silk (*kempu; kinu*)
NMAH-DT E4060, E4070, E4071?, E4072, E4076, E4091
W: 35.5–41.0 cm, L: 9 rolls (1 roll = ~2¹/₂ yards)

Description: *Kohaku hira-ori* or balanced plain weave silk taffeta with multicolored *kōshi-jima* 格子縞 (trellis pattern) in straight and tie-dyed plaid designs.

Characteristics: The straight plaids are without ikat, and the tie-dyed plaids have part of the warp and weft tie-dyed in the yarn (pers. comm. Fiske, letter, 24 October 1979). The individual colors and patterns are as follows: E4060 (41 cm wide), red, yellow, green, and white straight plaid; E4070 (35.5 cm wide), blue, ecru, and green straight plaid; E4071? (T18872 (86)) (35.5 cm wide), red, yellow, green, and white straight

NMAH-DT E4070

plaid; E4072 (41.0 cm wide), blue, yellow, and white straight plaid; E4076 (41.0 cm wide), red, green, blue, and white tie-dyed plaid; E4091 (41.0 cm wide), blue, gold, and ecru tie-dyed plaid. In the 18th century, the *dan'gawari* 段変り (lit. step-wise different; plaid) designed fabric was used mainly for theatrical costumes. The *atsuita* 厚板, a type of *nō* drama costume with a bold plaid design (Noma, 1974, figs. 183, pl. 13), was considered most suitable for actors playing the roles of strong characters (Noma, 1974:22, 183). Sometimes the plaids and stripes were combined in *nō* drama costume designs, thus creating the so-called *katami-gawari* 片身変り (lit. half the body different) type costume (Noma, 1974, fig. 64). Silk plaids and checks also gained popularity with *kabuki* actors, who were allowed to wear silk costumes after 1714 when the edict prohibiting the use of silk costumes was lifted (Shively, 1968:255, for the date). The *kōshi-jima* patterned fabrics, especially those with large-size main patterns, were one of the fabric designs frequently used for *yagu* 夜具 (bedding). Because *shima* 縞 refers both to stripes and plaids, these silk plaids are undoubtedly the famous silks of the Kai district (cf. entry 17, for information about Kai silks, donor, and various identifications).

Additional Specimens: E4087 (41.0 cm wide), red, yellow, green, and white straight plaid; E4088 (40.5 cm wide), same characteristics as E4060; E4092 (36.0 cm wide), brown, green, and white straight plaid.

NMAH-DT E4071?

NMAH-DT E4072

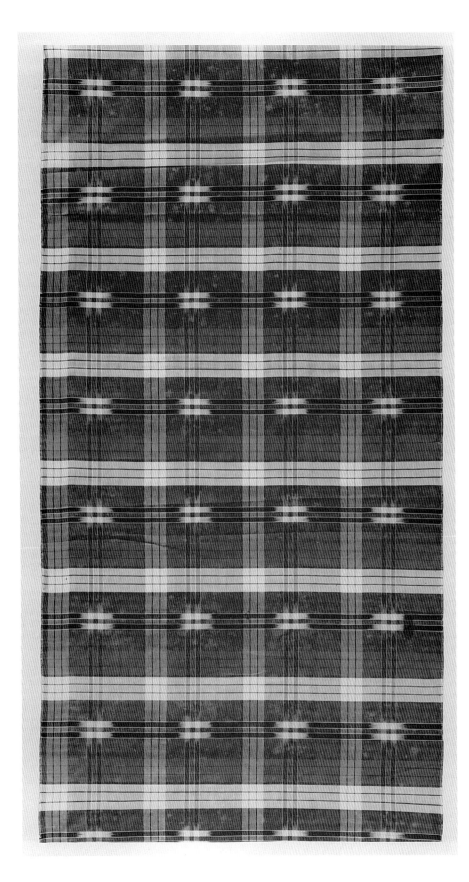

NMAH-DT E4076

NMAH-DT E4091

NMAH-DT E4069

19   Silk (*kempu; kinu*)
NMAH-DT E4069 (original no. ECC 224)
W: 41.0 cm, L: 1 roll (2¹/₂ yards)

Description: Plain weave silk taffeta.

Characteristics: This textile has evenly spaced red and white warp and weft stripes that produce a checkered pattern (pers. comm. Fiske, letter, 24 October 1979). Such checkered-pattern silk frequently was used as material for theatrical costumes (Noma, 1974, figs. 40, 108, 187, for early- and mid-Edo period *nō* drama costumes). The checkered pattern has been variously named *arare-mon* 霰文 (lit. hail pattern), which was of Egyptian origin and was introduced to Japan via China (Mori, 1969:18); *ishi-datami* 石畳 (lit. stone-mat; stones (pieces)) in a *go* 碁 (Japanese chess) board arrangement; and *ichimatsu* 市松 after the checkered-design costume worn on the occasion of the renouned 1741 performance by Sanogawa Ichimatsu 佐川市松 , a popular *kabuki* actor (*NKDJ*, 1976, volume 2, page 167; 1976, volume 9, page 109, for the origin; Noma, 1974: foldout 2, for the term included in "representative motifs" in Japanese textile designs). Checkered patterns generally are classed as *shima moyō*.

Remarks: This is a sample of silk from the Kai district (cf. entry 17, for a discussion of Japanese plain weave silks, their uses, donors of Kai silks, and various identifications).

NMAH-DT E4077 and E4078

20 Silk (*kempu; kinu*)
NMAH-DT E4077, E4078 (original nos. ECC 232, 233)
W: 15.0 cm, L: 2 rolls (1 roll = ~3 yards)

Description: Thin and soft *habutae* 羽二重 (lit. silk fabric only twice the weight of a feather, but not as soft), also called *tsumugi* 紬 (natural raw silk weave) or pongee fabric of Chinese origin, woven from raw silk.

Characteristics: E4077 is dyed red; ECC E4078 is in ecru (natural white). The smoothness of *habutae* fabric is the result of what is known as the *kome-ori* 穀織 (lit. grain weave) technique, a type of twill weave (pers. comm. Fiske, letter, 24 October 1979). Because of its thin, silky softness, it was widely used for ceremonial garments, feminine apparel, and the linings of special fineries (*NKDJ,* 1976, volume 16, page 406, for various uses). The shogunal government presented 20 *tan* (roll) of red and 5 *tan* of white pongee (1 *tan* = ~12 yards) to the United States and to Commodore Perry, respectively, at Kanagawa in March 1854. As is well known, the offering of cloth, especially silk, has ceremonial significance (cf. entry 17).

Remarks: These two rolls of silk have been variously identified as "pongee" in the HNL and PJL (cf. Appendixes I, II), "habutae" in the NGL (*BGKM,* 1912, volume 4, page 557), "*kenchū*" 繭紬 (variant of *habutae*) in HL (Hora, 1970:241–242), and "*nuno*" 光絹 (lit. soft and shiny silk) in the KORL (*BGKM,* 1914, volume 5, page 311). They were entered simply as "silk" in the 1859-ACB, 1953-AL, and USNM-ECC, and as "plain silk" in the NMAH-DT catalog.

21 Silk (*kempu; kinu*)
NMAH-DT E4103–E4106 (original nos. ECC 258, 260, 263, ?)
W: 44.5–49.0 cm, L: 4 rolls (1 roll = ~68 cm)

Description: Silk *chirimen* 縮緬 (lit. fabric with crinkled surface; crepe de chine) woven with single thread warp and multiple twisted threads weft that is heat treated after weaving.

Characteristics: These silks are examples of *itajime* 板締 (block resist print), stencil dyed, figured silk in floral and geometric weave (pers. comm. Fiske, letter, 24 October 1979). E4103 (44.5 cm wide) has a pattern of roundels with floral sprays of *shōchikikubai* (pine, bamboo, and plum) and *kanoko* 鹿子 (eye pattern; spots on young deer's coat; tie-dyed spotted pattern) that are effected in white on a red ground. The compact arrangement of *kanoko* design within roundels resembles the effect of tie-dyeing. E4104 (48.0 cm wide) is a salmon color silk crepe in warp-float weave (pers. comm. Fiske, letter, 24 October 1979). The overall design is of rows of *shōchikikubai* arranged against vertical serpentine lines creating what is called *tatewaku* 立涌 (vertical seething) design. E4105 (44.5 cm wide) is an ivory silk crepe in weft-float weave (pers. comm. Fiske, letter, 24 October 1979) with an overall chrysanthemum floral design. E4106 (49.0 cm wide) is a blue silk crepe in damask weave (pers. comm. Fiske, letter, 24 October 1994) with a design of an overall fret pattern or *sayagata* 綾型 (linked swastikas) design. The *itajime* is the stencil dyeing method by which the fabric is folded and clamped between two thin stenciled boards in a decorative design. The dye is applied to cut-out portions. The design is sometimes cut in only one of the two boards to create the desired effect (Okada, 1958:9; *NKDJ,* 1976, volume 2, page 103, for the *itajime* technique of stencil dyeing). The *chirimen* weaving technique is said to have been introduced to Japan in the late 16th century by Chinese weavers (cf. entry 17, for other types of silk weave introduced by the Chinese). The *chirimen* fabric is used mainly for clothing, such as, kimono, belts, jacket linings, etc., but it also is suitable for *furoshiki* 風呂敷 (square wrapping cloth) (*NKDJ,* 1976, volume 13, page 582, for popular uses).

Remarks: These silks were entered in the HNL as "5 pieces flowered crape, 5 pieces red dyed figured crape" for the Government of the United States, and "2 pieces flowered crape, 3 pieces figured dyed crape" presented to Commodore Perry at

NMAH-DT E4103

Kanagawa in March 1854 (cf. Appendix I). They were identified in HL as "*mon chirimen*" 紋縮緬 (figured *chirimen*) and "*itajime chirimen*" (block resist stencil dyed *chirimen*) (Hora, 1970:241). Perry received five additional bolts (~60 yards) of crepe de chine at Shimoda in June 1854 (cf. Appendix III). These were entered as "assorted pieces of silk" in the 1859-ACB and 1953-AL, and as "chirimen" (Japanese silk crepe) in the ECC and NMNH-DT catalogs. E4103 was renumbered as T4103 by the Division of Textiles, Smithsonian Institution.

NMAH-DT E4104

NMAH-DT E4105

NMAH-DT E4106

NMAH-DT E4110 (top), E4111 (bottom)

22 Cotton fabric (*mempu* 綿布 ; *momen* 木綿)
NMAH-DT E4110, E4111 (original nos. ECC 264, 265)
W: 34.5 cm, L: two rolls (1 yard each)

Description: *Kata-zome* 型染 or hand-painted, resist dyed cotton fabric in balanced, plain weave.

Characteristics: Resist rice paste is hand applied on linear portions of the stencil designs and dyed in blue to achieve the shade of background coloring. Additional indigo and grey colors are applied by hand before washing out the resist substance (for paste-resist variations see Nakano, 1982:113–123). E4110 has a combination of floral and geometric designs

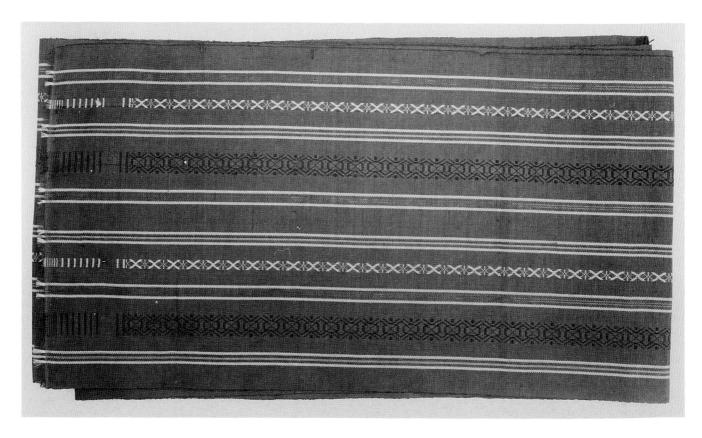

USNM ECC 27

of circles and stylized squares in black, grey, and white on indigo blue. E4111 is a floral design that consists of cherry blossoms, bellflowers, maple leaves, and pine sprigs in black, grey, and white against indigo blue. Both fabric designs are representative of *aigata* 藍型 (basically indigo blue fabric with added coloring of shades of blue, grey, and black) (Hauge and Hauge, 1978:254, for the term, coloring, and the method of dyeing). The monochrome stencil dyeing technique using relatively small patterns on silk is said to have been developed in the late 16th century and, by the 18th century, the multicolored, stenciled cotton fabrics came to be used exclusively by commoners for clothing, bedding, and other materials (Hauge and Hauge, 1978:27–28; Blakemore, 1978: 8–11; Tuer, 1967:16–19, for details of dyeing techniques). Especially in the Ryūkyūan tradition, *aigata* fabrics with fine patterns were used exclusively by the common people for garments and other everyday-use items (Okamura, 1946:18, plate 3, for illustration).

Remarks: Three rolls of blue cotton fabrics were received from the Regent and the Treasurers of the Kingdom of Ryūkyū at Naha in July 1854. They were entered as *"konji momen nuno"* 紺地木綿布 (indigo cotton fabric) in the Ryūkyūan gift list (cf. Appendixes IIIB, IIID) but were identified as assorted Japanese cotton pieces in the 1859-ACB and 1953-AL and as "printed cotton cloth" in the ECC.

Additional Specimens: E4112 is a *kasuri* 耕；飛白 (splashed pattern) or double ikat, thread tie-dyed, indigo blue fabric in geometric design that results in alternating columns in small rectangles (pers. comm. Fiske, letter, 24 October 1979).

23 Belt (obi 帯)
USNM ECC 27
W: 18.7 cm, L: 557.3 cm

Description: Hakata-ori 博多織 (pers. comm. Cort, conversation, 2 September 1983; Stinchecum, letter, 7 December 1980), a man's belt made of plain weave, warp-faced blue silk, with warp-floats in light and dark brown geometric patterns.

Characteristics: Such belts are worn folded double over an outer robe. Hakata, which now forms part of the port city of Fukuoka 福岡, Kyūshū 九州, was one of the most important trading ports and was noted for its silk industry. The

USNM ECC 292

Hakata-ori, or the Hakata weave, was introduced from China during the Tembun 天文 period (1532–1555); therefore, it also is called Hakata *kara-ori* 唐織 (Chinese weave) (for history and term see *NKDJ,* 1976, volume 16, page 149).

Remarks: The belt probably was received at Naha, Ryūkyūs, as an informal gift (USNM-ECC), but it was not included in any of official lists of gifts. It was on view in the exhibit, "Navy, Science, Diplomacy, and Exploration," at the NMAH until November 1989.

24 Decorated letter paper (*moyō zuri bensen* 模様刷便箋 ; *hōsho e hankiri* 奉書絵半切)
USNM ECC 292–296
L: 17.5 cm, W: 48 cm (~600 sheets in 10 packets)

Description: White, thick, and absorbent *hōsho* letter paper, handmade of *kōzo* 楮 (paper mulberry pulp) mixed with rice powder and a daphne or laurel root fixative (Joya, 1958:25, for ingredients used), especially suitable for brush writing.

Characteristics: The paper is decorated with colored woodblock prints chiefly of floral and other designs from nature as follows: ECC 292, peony, daffodil, chrysanthemum, and cherry blossoms mainly in red but with additional yellow, pink, and green coloring; ECC 293, bamboo in black and white; ECC 294, chrysanthemums in yellow, rose, green, and white; ECC 295, ocean waves in light blue; and ECC 296, cherry blossoms in pink. *Hōsho* or *hōsho-gami* 奉書紙 (*hōsho* paper) refers to "high quality paper" in contemporary usage. It is said

to have been so named as early as the 16th century when this type of paper was used exclusively by the emperor and court officials in writing important edicts and memorials. Because such documents were considered sacred, *hōsho* (lit. sacred or official document) eventually came to be synonymous with high grade letter paper (Joya, 1958:24, for origin of the term; *NKDJ,* 1976, volume 18, pages 44–45, for history of its various usages). These samples were manufactured by Imai Handayū 今井半太夫 of Atami 熱海 (city), Zushū 豆州 (Izu district, modern Shizuoka prefecture), and were distributed by the Kinkadō Sugiharaya 金花堂杉原屋 stationery shop in Edo [modern Tokyo]. The stationer's descriptive listing, *gampishi mokuroku* 雁皮紙目録 (catalog of *gampi* paper), of various merchandise is included in several of the packets. The *gampishi* is handmade of specially treated *Wikstroemia gampi* pulp and is prized for qualities of strength and softness (Joya, 1958:44, for details of the paper-making process, a 7th century importation from Korea).

Remarks: Five boxes of decorated letter paper were presented by the senior reception commissioner, Hayashi Daigaku-no-kashira, at Kanagawa in March 1854 (HL; KORL; NGL). They were variously identified as "*hōsho e hankiri*" (decorated letter paper) in the NGL (*BGKM,* 1912, volume 4, page 559); "*saiga ori kanshi*" 彩画折筒紙 (painted, folding letter paper) in the KORL (*BGKM,* 1914, volume 5, page 314); "*moyōzuri bensen*" (letter paper with printed decoration) (Hora, 1970:242); and "stamped note and letter paper" and "stamped note paper" in the HNL and PJL, respectively (cf. Appendixes I, II).

USNM ECC 293

USNM ECC 294

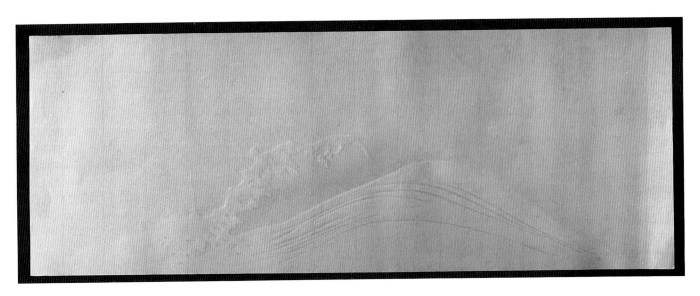

USNM ECC 295

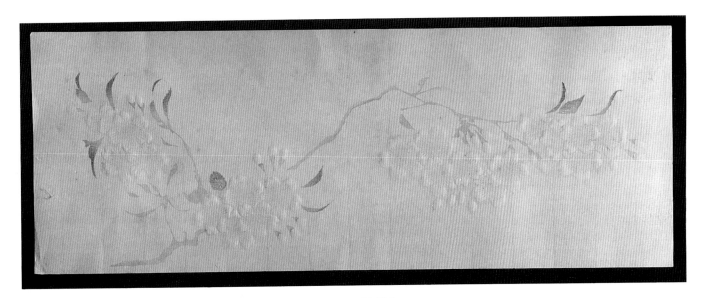

USNM ECC 296

USNM ECC 297a–c

for various uses). The choice of five colors may represent a Japanese adaptation of the Chinese concept of five primary colors: black, red, blue, white, and yellow. They are believed to symbolize the five elements (water, fire, wood, metal, and earth), the principal active constituents of nature. In East Asian traditions, the numeral five is particularly felicitous (Williams, 1976:186, 295, for symbolism). A strip of paper that appears to have been used to bundle the five separate packets carries a label (4 × 6.5 cm) bordered with a gold floral design. The label reads: "*gyoei zōshi*" 御詠草紙 (note paper for poetry writing by nobles of the imperial court) (*NKDJ*, 1976, volume 6, page 216; 1976, volume 12, page 265, for definition). Probably the same maker of the decorated letter paper made the strip, and most likely they all were sold by the same stationer (cf. entry 24).

Remarks: The paper was presented by Hayashi at Kanagawa in March 1854. The KORL identifies the item as "*gosaisen*" 五彩箋 (note paper painted in five colors) (*BGKM*, 1914, volume 5, page 314); they were erroneously identified as "*hana moyō gami*" 花模様紙 (paper with floral design) (Hora, 1970:242) and as "flowered note paper" in the HNL and PJL, respectively (cf. Appendixes I, II).

25 Writing paper in five colors (*goshiki hōsho-shi* 五色奉書紙 or *hōsho-gami*)
USNM ECC 297a–e
L: 49.5 cm, W: 26 cm (42 sheets; nine sheets per packet, except one packet of six sheets)

Description: Thick, soft paper in green (ECC 297a), red (ECC 297b), violet [faded black] (ECC 297c), white (ECC 297d), and deep yellow (ECC 297e), all with faint traces of sprayed gold dust.

Characteristics: The *hōsho* type of handmade paper (cf. entry 24 for the special materials required in paper making, its history, associated attributes, etc.) is used for writing formal and ceremonial notes and also for gift wrapping (Joya, 1958:24,

26 Paper (*kami* 紙)
USNM ECC 298 (not illustrated)
L: 32 cm, W: 27.5 cm

Description: A sheet of *minogami* 美濃紙 (lit. paper produced in the province of Mino (modern Gifu prefecture)).

Characteristics: This paper is an off-white, buff colored grainy paper made of mulberry fibers mixed with rice powder, which was used for brush writing, papering windows, wrapping objects including gifts, and for other varied purposes because of its strength and high absorbency.

Remarks: The paper was received from the chief commissioner, Hayashi. In the HNL, it is described simply as "one box of paper" (cf. Appendix I), whereas the HL identifies the size and type of paper as being "*Dai-mino-gami*" 大美濃紙 (large sheet of mino-gami)" (Hora, 1970:242), as does the Japanese NGL (*BGKM*, 1912, volume 4, page 559).

Ceramics

27 Pottery vase (*hana-ike* 花生け ; *kabin* 花瓶)
USNM ECC 106
H: 22 cm, D: 11 cm

Description: *Fujina-yaki* 布志名焼 flower vase in cylindrical form.

Characteristics: The straight sides are slightly shouldered below a short straight neck with everted rim. Vertical loop handles are fixed on either side at the shoulder. The light fawn, baked clay body is glazed both inside and outside in dull, dark brown, and additional maroon and gold glaze extends from the bottom upward in bold streaks. The entire body is overpainted with such traditional, auspicious designs as *unkaku* 雲鶴 (flying cranes and clouds) in maroon, orange, and green, and *kiri* 桐 (paulownia) blossoms symbolic of power and nobility (Dower, 1971:68–69, for legendary and historic significance of *kiri* design and its varied renderings), which are rendered in gold and maroon. The shoulder is decorated with an overglaze Greek key scroll in olive green, and the neck has a modified key pattern in green, enclosed in blue triangles. *Fujina-yaki* pottery was produced at Fujina in the Izumo 出雲 district (modern Shimane prefecture) (Kato, 1972:845). On the bottom of the vase and encircled by a double ring is the stamped pottery mark used for *Fujina-yaki:* "Izumo Jyakuzan" 出雲若山 (Kato, 1972:55, for identical pottery marks in a single ring; Morse, 1901:161, gives the reading as Izumo Takuzan in error). Also on the bottom is stamped "Dai Nippon" 大日本 in a square. It was manufactured ca. 1830–1844 for export (Kato, 1972:845, for dating; Morse, 1901:159, for identification as a typical Fujina pottery made as export ware).

Remarks: This piece is very likely from Ido Iwami-no-kami because both the Iwami and Izumo districts are in modern Shimane prefecture.

USNM ECC 106

USNM ECC 285

28 Pottery teapot (*dobin* 土瓶 ; *chabin* 茶瓶 ; *chadashi* 茶出し)
USNM ECC 285
H: 9.8 cm, D: 14 cm

Description: Pottery with a dark brown glaze on hard fired grey body in the shape of a slightly bevelled teapot.

Characteristics: The teapot has a knobbed, convex cover, a conical side spout, and three small (1 cm high) feet. This shape is known as "Satsuma" 薩摩 shape, and such teapots are invariably Satsuma teapots (Cort, 1979:231, 263, for particular types of Kyūshū teapots). A thin, brass handle is ornamented with incised diagonal crosses and *futatsu-tomoe* 二つ巴絵 (two comma shapes so united as to make a circle) design circles.

Remarks: The piece is unmarked. It probably was a purchased item or an informal gift, as none of the official lists of Japanese presents includes a pottery teapot. There is an entry for "*yakimono rui*" 焼物類 (pottery ware) in the AWL (*BGKM,* 1914, volume 6, page 198).

USNM ECC 107

29 Porcelain cake jar (*kashi-bachi* 菓子鉢)
USNM ECC 107
H: 17.5 cm, D: 26 cm

Description: Blue and white Arita 有田 ware, lidded porcelain jar for storing cakes, sweetmeats, and other confectioneries.

Characteristics: The cylindrical body has an extended foot rim and a shallow, inverted, saucer-like lid with a protruding rim. The exterior is decorated with a design pattern of cranes in flight, which are auspicious symbols of longevity (Edmunds, 1934:316–317; Dower, 1971:90–91, especially for various patterns of Japanese uses of the crane-design motif). A stylized geometric wave pattern, also in underglaze blue, encircles the lower third of the body just above the foot rim.

Remarks: This probably is one of the seven blue and white porcelain wares presented by Ido and Izawa at Shimoda in June 1854 (*BGKM,* 1914, volume 6, page 311, for KORL entry: "*shino utsuwa*" 青花瓷器 (early blue and white Imari porcelain)). It was exhibited in "The Japan Expedition 1852–1855 of Commodore Matthew Calbraith Perry," Smithsonian Institution, Washington, D.C., in 1968.

Top row, from left to right: USNM ECC 202, ECC 204, ECC 206
Bottom row, from left to right: USNM ECC 201, ECC 203, ECC 205

30 Wine cup (*sakazuki* 酒杯)
USNM ECC 205
H: 3 cm, D: 6.3 cm

Description: Hemispherical *sake* 酒 cup in eggshell porcelain with a painted gold rim and a shallow footring banded with a fret design in blue.

Characteristics: The inside of the cup contains an overglaze enamel painting in relief of the sacred Mt. Fuji outlined in black and shaded with grey and green. At the base of the mountain, the figure of a golden dragon emerges from black clouds. The inscription with the artist's red seal mark reads: "Seiun *sha* 晴雲写 , *baigetsu* or *umetsuki sha*" 梅月写 (painted by Seiun in the second month of the lunar calendar (*umetsuki*; lit. the plum month)). Morse (1901:105) illustrates a Baigetsu *ga* 梅月画 mark on a piece of pottery from the Province of Ise. Katō (1972:771) also identifies *baigetsu* as an Ise 伊勢 *kobanko* 古万古 (ko = old, banko = a type of ware produced at the Banko Kiln in Ise) ware mark. The potter's underglaze mark in faint blue on the bottom of the cup reads: "*fuku*" 福 (good fortune).

Remarks: This wine cup (one of six such cups) was presented by Hayaski to the United States at Kanagawa, March 1854. It is included in the KORL (*BGKM,* 1914, volume 5, pages 308, 315), and the HNL and PJL list them simply as cups (cf. Appendexes I, II).

31 Wine cup (*sakazuki*)
USNM ECC 204
H: 3 cm, D: 6.3 cm

Description: Hemispherical, eggshell porcelain *sake* cup with a painted gold rim and a shallow footring bordered with a fret design in blue.

Characteristics: The inside of the cup is decorated with an overglaze enamel painting in relief of a carp, in gold and black, swimming up a waterfall. The waterfall is suggested by faint green ripples; black rocks and green plants are in the background. The inscription accompanying the artist's red seal reads: "Hōei *sha*" 宝栄写 (painted by Hōei). The bottom of the cup carries an illegible potter's underglaze mark in faint blue.

Remarks: This wine cup (one of six such cups) was presented by Hayaski to the United States at Kanagawa, March 1854. It is included in the KORL (*BGKM,* 1914, volume 5, pages 308, 315), and the HNL and PJL list them simply as cups (cf. Appendexes I, II).

32 Wine cup (*sakazuki*)
USNM ECC 203
H: 3 cm, D: 6.3 cm

Description: Hemispherical *sake* cup in eggshell porcelain with a low footring.

Characteristics: The footring is decorated with a Greek fret design in underglaze blue, whereas the inside of the cup is decorated with blue enamel in relief in the traditional *shōchikubai* design. Additional decorative features include the gilded rim, gold speckles amidst tree branches and leaves, and the painter's red seal marks. A faint blue potter's mark in underglaze is on the bottom of the cup.

Remarks: This wine cup (one of six such cups) was presented by Hayaski to the United States at Kanagawa, March 1854. It is included in the KORL (*BGKM,* 1914, volume 5, pages 308, 315), and the HNL and PJL list them simply as cups (cf. Appendexes I, II).

33 Wine cup (*sakazuki*)
USNM ECC 202
H: 3 cm, Dia 6.3 cm

Description: Hemispherical, eggshell porcelain *sake* cup with a low footring banded with a fret design in underglaze blue.

Characteristics: The cup's interior is ornamented with an enamelled relief painting of a flying crane in black against a crimson sun and gilded clouds. A black inscription reads: "Seiun *sha* Baigetsu or *umetsuki sha*" (cf. entry 30 for the identical inscription). Although the decorator's seal mark is in red, there also is a faint blue potter's mark in underglaze on the bottom of the cup declaring "*fuku*" (good fortune).

Remarks: This wine cup (one of six such cups) was presented by Hayaski to the United States at Kanagawa, March 1854. It is included in the KORL (*BGKM,* 1914, volume 5, pages 308, 315), and the HNL and PJL list them simply as cups (cf. Appendexes I, II).

34 Wine cup (*sakazuki*)
USNM ECC 206
H: 3 cm, D: 6.3 cm

Description: Hemispherical *sake* drinking cup, in eggshell porcelain, with gold painted rim and a shallow footring banded with a fret design in blue.

Characteristics: Inside the cup is an overglaze enamel painting, in relief, of a peony blossom and a butterfly, both in black with added colors of grey, green, and gold. The inscriptions in black, accompanied by the artist's red seal mark, read: "Kuniiro" 国色 (name of the artist?) "*hyakkaō*" 百花王 (lit. the king of all flowers; a classical variant of *botan,* peony). The potter's underglaze mark in faint blue is on the bottom of the cup.

Remarks: This wine cup (one of six such cups) was presented by Hayaski to the United States at Kanagawa, March 1854. It is included in the KORL (*BGKM,* 1914, volume 5, pages 308, 315), and the HNL and PJL list them simply as cups (cf. Appendexes I, II).

35 Wine cup (*sakazuki*)
USNM ECC 201
H: 3 cm, D: 6.3 cm

Description: Hemispherical *sake* cup in eggshell porcelain with a low footring.

Characteristics: The interior of the cup is ornamented with an overglaze enamel painting in relief of irises and sparrows in blue. The Greek fret design, also in blue relief, decorates the inside border beneath the gold rim. Gold speckles and a red painter's seal mark are added.

Remarks: This wine cup (one of six such cups) was presented by Hayaski to the United States at Kanagawa, March 1854. It is included in the KORL (*BGKM,* 1914, volume 5, pages 308, 315), and the HNL and PJL list them simply as cups (cf. Appendexes I, II).

USNM ECC 172 (left) and ECC 176 (right)

36   Covered pottery tea jar? (chaki 茶器 ?; choka 茶家 ?)
USNM ECC 176
H: 6.7 cm, D: 7 cm

Description: Lidded Seto 瀬戸 ware *dō-bari* 胴張 type ceramic box. Identifiable as *dō-bari* by it cylindrical, slightly convex shape (BT, 1982:170).

Characteristics: Both the inside and outside surfaces of the thin, hard, sandy grey body are unevenly covered with dark brown glaze and scattered splotches of light brown (Boger, 1964:232–234, for description of the characteristics of Seto ware; Swann, 1958:111–112, for the history). The lid fits inside the slightly convex, sharply shouldered mouth of the box. The inside of the lid is grey and was left unglazed. The raised potter's mark, "Shingō" 信號 , is stamped on the bottom. This box may be a *choka* (cf. Appendixes IIIB, IIID), which typically was used in Ryūkyū to store powdered tea; however, Cort's opinion (letter, 7 December 1982) is that its use may be varied, but that it certainly was not used for tea.

Remarks: This jar probably was part of the official Ryūkyūan gifts received at Naha in July 1854.

Additional Specimens: ECC 134, 135, and 174 (cover missing) are identical to ECC 176.

37   Covered pottery tea jar ? (chaki ?)
USNM ECC 172
H: 10.5 cm, D: 12 cm

Description: Cylindrical, lidded Seto ware type ceramic box.

Characteristics: The box is essentially the same as entry 36, except for size.

Additional Specimens: ECC 171, 173.

USNM ECC 282

38 Pottery water pitcher (*mizu sashi* 水差し)
USNM ECC 282
H: 25.5 cm, D: 16.4 cm

Description: Ovoid body with a wide, short neck, conical spout, convex knobbed cover, and fixed bail.

Characteristics: The exterior is ornamented with black *nagashi-gusuri* 流釉 (a glaze that is poured on, creating irregular flowing patterns), and the bail, cover, and the upper part of the body have a green drip glaze that shows some brush strokes. This is a good example of black Satsuma ware with a thin transparent glaze that covers the surface of the hard-fired, reddish clay. The pottery is unmarked.

Remarks: This probably was received from the regent of the Kingdom of Ryūkyū at Naha in July 1854 (cf. Appendix IIIB; Hickman and Fetchko, 1977, entry 241, for a similar specimen acquired at Naha prior to 1888). It was identified as an "erthen kettle" in the 1859-ACB and 1953-AL, but it was entered in the ECC as a "pottery teapot" and there identified as a ceramic ware of southern Kyūshū origin.

USNM ECC 156

39　Porcelain lantern (*tōrō* 灯籠)
USNM ECC 156
H: 79 cm, D: 26 cm

Description: Stupa-shape, white, Arita porcelain temple lantern (Janata, 1965, entry 73, for a similar specimen identified as a temple lantern in the shape of a stupa) decorated with underglaze blue and overglaze enamel paintings in dark vermilion and gold as in traditional *Imari sansai* 伊万里三彩 (blue, red, and gold or Imari export porcelain) color combinations.

Characteristics: The lantern consists of three separate parts: (1) a columnar pillar on a hexagonal base; (2) a round light box with four panels of floral openwork; and (3) an hexagonal roof-shape cover with an ovoid peak that is held in place by three flame-like openwork clasps. The main ornamentation includes conventional auspicious motifs, such as, *nami ni chidori* 波に千鳥 (birds over waves), clouds, a dragon, and blossoms of peony, plum, chrysanthemum, and lotus that are accented by *hanabishi* 花菱 (floral lozenges), *shippo tsunagi* しっぽつなぎ (joined, interlocking circles), and *karakusa* 唐草 (lit. Chinese grass; arabesque) geometric patterns. The obvious religious features are the egg-shape apex of the roof that represents a "precious jewel" or a "fabulous pearl," and the openwork "flames of fire" clasps that secure it. Porcelain *tōrō* of this type are placed on the altar of Buddhist temples as offerings, but they also are used for lighting during nocturnal rites and services (Joya, 1958:36, 93–94, for uses of temple lanterns; Newman and Ryerson, 1964:64, for the origin of Buddhist lanterns as votive offerings).

Remarks: This probably is one of seven various types of blue and white porcelain wares that was presented by Ido and Izawa as additional gifts at Shimoda in June 1854. The SGL entry reads: "*shi no utsuwa*" (early blue and white porcelain ware) (*BGKM,* 1914, volume 6, page 311).

USNM ECC 198

USNM ECC 125

40 Stoneware tea cup (*chawan* 茶椀)
USNM ECC 198
H: 5 cm, D: 8.1 cm

Description: Bowl-shape tea cup sloping inward from the rim to the footring.

Characteristics: The cup has molded decoration done with 13 panels having contiguous facets that end in an irregular octagonal pattern. There are fine crackles on the creamy greyish buff color glaze on both the inside and outside of the bowl. The bowl is unmarked.

Remarks: Probably this cup was one of the cups received from Hayashi Daigaku-no-kashira (Hora, 1970:242, for the entry for "*chawan*"). Both the PJL and the HNL record cups as being gifts from Hayashi, but they do not give information regarding their specific types. The OSL of official gifts (Appendixes IIIB, IIID) includes "*dō chawan san-soku*" 上焼茶椀三束 (3 bundles of high quality tea cups). This cup may be part of the Ryūkyūan gifts.

Additional Specimens: ECC 131-133, 195-197, 199, 200. The number of panels per cup ranges from 12 to 17.

41 Porcelain noodle-sauce cup (*choko* 猪口; *choko-hai* 猪口盃; *choku* 猪口)
USNM ECC 125
H: 7.5 cm, D: 8.3 cm

Description: White and underglaze blue Imari ware cylindrical porcelain cup used for serving *soba* 蕎麦 (buckwheat noodles) sauce.

Characteristics: Cups such as this also were used as serving vessels for tea, wine, and other liquids, depending upon the cup size and the given occasion (Hauge, 1978:243). During manufacture, the cup was thrown on its sides, thereby creating shallow, vertical panels that circle the center of the cup. The vertical panels slope slightly inward to the footring. This cup definitely is a late Edo period *choko* specimen in body form and size (Sera, 1959:72-74, for commentary and illustrated dating chart for the various *choko* forms that evolved from the Ming import tea cup in the early 17th century), which resembles a contemporary *yunomi chawan* 湯飲茶椀 (teacup). It is decorated with a geometrical *hanabishi* design in a wide band just below the rim. A seascape, with mountains, trees, and cottages in the background, lies beneath the band. Additional ornamentation includes a band of alternating diagonal crosses and circles above the footring, and the interior rim is banded with a meandering design. The potter's mark in underglaze blue on the bottom reads: "Yamaguchi" [山口], which is probably the potter's name or the name of the kiln.

Remarks: Although the HNL notes "2 boxes porcelain cups" as items received from Udono and "3 boxes porcelain goblets" from Matsuzaki, this *choko* probably was presented by Matsuzaki because its size and form approximates what westerners then called a "goblet" (*BGKM*, 1912, volume 4, page 556; Hora, 1970:242, for entries for "*chokohai*" in the list of Japanese presents).

Additional Specimens: ECC 126, 127, 183-188. All are identical to ECC 125.

USNM ECC 128

42   Porcelain noodle-sauce cup (*choko; choko-hai; choku*)
USNM ECC 128
H: 7.5 cm, D: 8.1 cm

Description: Blue and white Imari porcelain, cylindrical cup on a low footring, used for serving *soba* sauce.

Characteristics: Cups such as this also were used as serving vessels for other liquids (cf. entry 41 for the varied uses, sizes, and forms). The interior is white whereas the exterior is solidly colored in underglaze deep blue. A modified Greek key design band in light blue decorates the inside, just below the rim. The potter's mark in blue seal character on the bottom reads: "Yamaguchi" 山口 .

Remarks: This *choko* was presented by Matsuzaki. Its size and form approximates what westerners then called a "goblet." The HNL lists "3 boxes porcelain goblets" (Hawks, 1856:369, for entry; see also *BGKM,* 1912, volume 4, page 556, and Hora, 1970:242, for entries for "*choko-hai*" in the list of Japanese presents).

Additional Specimens: ECC 129, 130, 189–192. All are identical to ECC 128.

USNM ECC 105 (two views)

43 Porcelain water jar (*mizubachi* 水鉢 ; *chōzubachi* 丁子鉢)
USNM ECC 105
H: 34.5 cm, D: 33.7 cm

Description: White and underglaze blue Arita ware *mizubachi* in globular form with slightly voluted sides and a short, straight neck with everted rim.

Characteristics: The jar is ornamented with such traditional, auspicious designs as the bat (symbol of good fortune from an etymological contortion), a legendary immortal plant known as an elixir of life, *agemaki* 揚巻 (a decorative, tied cord), a cloud, the moon, maple and bamboo leaves, berries, and the most prominent of all, peony blossoms. The rim, neck, and lower base are decorated with bands of cross-hatching saw teeth and other geometric patterns. The jar is unmarked.

Remarks: This jar is probably the one with *fukuju* 福寿 (good fortune and longevity) design, which was listed as one of the seven types of blue and white porcelain ware presented by Ido Tsushima-no-kami and Izawa Mimasaka-no-kami (*BGKM*, 1914, volume 6, page 311, for entry "*shi no utsuwa*"; cf. Appendix III). The Ryūkyūan official gift list also includes ceramic water jars (OSL, 1982:544; cf. Appendixes IIIB, IIID).

USNM ECC 108

44 Porcelain planter (*ueki-bachi* 植木鉢 *hanaike* 花生け)
USNM ECC 108
L: 37.5 cm, W: 25.5 cm, H: 12.5 cm

Description: Broad, shallow, rectangular vessel in white and underglaze blue porcelain, raised on four decorated feet, and used for *bonsai* 盆栽 (dwarf-tree culture) (Roger, 1964:199–200, for uses) or *moribana* 盛花 (floral or plant arrangement).

Characteristics: The flat rim extends outward and is ornamented with the meandering pattern, the symbolical equivalent of thunder, which represents fecundity and the basic forces of life (Laufer, 1902:41; and Dower, 1971:40, for symbolism). Scattered flowers, butterflies, and *mizugaki* 瑞垣 (lit. sacred fence; trellis) pattern (or a stylized basket-weave design) decorate the front and back; the *unkaku* design (flying cranes amid clouds, symbolizing longevity and fertility or elegance and happiness) is used on the two side panels. The base is unglazed and bears no mark.

Remarks: This probably is one of the seven items entered under "*shi no utsuwa*" as additional gifts presented at Shimoda from Ido Tsushima-no-kami and Izawa Mimasaka-no-kami (SGL in *BGKM*, 1914, volume 6, page 311). The HNL entries for porcelain vessels are listed as "porcelain cups" and "porcelain goblets" and are listed as being received from Udono Mimbu Shōyū and Matsuzaki Mitsutarō.

45 Large porcelain dish (*ōzara* 大皿)
USNM ECC 103
H: 12.5 cm, D: 62 cm

Description: Large, shallow Imari ware serving dish in *sometsuke* 染付 (white and underglaze blue) porcelain.

Characteristics: A traditional auspicious *shōchikubai* design of pine, bamboo, and plum blossoms (called the "three companions of the cold," which symbolize longevity and endurance) decorates the central panel, which is encircled with a band of flower petals and reciprocal triangles. The remaining area of the interior is ornamented with *kanoko botan* 鹿子牡丹 design (minute white spots amid clusters of peony petals, giving a dappled effect, often used on tie-dyed fabrics) (Dower, 1971:23, for various uses of *kanoko* as a decorative motif; *BGKM*, 1916, volume 8, page 540, for the term). The outer surface is decorated with *warabide* わらび手 design (lit. hand of bracken, symbolizing early spring) (Dower, 1971:50), and figures of plum blossoms are interspersed. A band of alternately arranged circles and diagonal crosses covers the area near the foot rim. The imprint at the bottom within a single ring reads: "*Tai Min Seika-nen sei*" 太明成化年製 (manufactured [in imitation of] the Ming dynasty Ch'eng-hua period [1465–1487] blue and white porcelain known as *seika-ki* 成化器) (Kato, 1972:511). It probably was manufactured ca. 1800 (Shugio, 1896:56). At Arita, the Japanese produced a series of porcelains for export by the Dutch East

USNM ECC 103 (side view)

USNM ECC 103 (top view)

USNM ECC 104 (side view)

India Company (Stitt, 1974:11; Young 1973:215; Shugio, 1896, entry 228, for the identical mark; also Knapp and Atil, 1975, volume 10, plate 61; Garner, 1955:77, for dating and attribution).

Remarks: The dish was presented by Ido Tsushima-no-kami who represented one of the historically renown kiln districts, Tsushima (modern Nagasaki prefecture). The entry "*gokujō yakimono chawan-zara, sometsuke ōzara shōchikubai kanoko botan, nimai*" 極上焼物茶碗皿染付大皿 松竹梅鹿子牡丹 二枚 (top quality blue and white porcelain cups and dishes, including two large dishes with *shōchikubai* and *kanoko botan* decoration) appears in both the SML (in *BGKM,* 1916, volume 8, page 540) and the SGL (in *BGKM,* 1914, volume 6, page 311).

46 Large porcelain dish (*ōzara*)
USNM ECC 104
H: 12.5 cm, D: 62 cm

Description: Large, shallow Imari ware serving dish in *sometsuke* porcelain.

Characteristics: The interior center is ornamented with *shōchikubai* design encircled by a band of interlocking triangles. The remainder of the inside surface is decorated with snail-like spirals commonly known as *tako-karakusa* 章魚唐草 (octopus arabesque) pattern (pers. comm. Hauge, letter, 23 July 1992), and the entire outside surface is decorated with interlaced *warabide* design. On the underside of the bowl is an imprint within a single circle, which reads: "*Tai Min Seika-nen sei.*" It probably was made ca. 1800 (Shugio, 1896:56, see entry 228 for the identical mark). For other detailed references regarding pottery marks on Japanese blue and white export ware, see the discussion for ECC 103, entry 45.

Remarks: The dish was received from Ido Tsushima-no-kami at Shimoda in June 1854 (SML in *BGKM,* 1916, volume 8, page 540; SGL in *BGKM,* 1914, volume 6, page 311).

USNM ECC 104 (top view)

Fans, Umbrellas, and Tobacco Pipes

USNM ECC 290e

47 Fan (*sensu* 扇子 ; *ōgi* 扇)
USNM ECC 290e
L: 28.6 cm, W: ~40 cm (top when unfolded)

Description: Folding fan made of paper and bamboo.

Characteristics: Oiled, white mulberry bark paper is pasted to the front and back sides of 10 flat bamboo ribs, which are fastened at the bottom with a steel *kaname* 要 (rivet) at the base. The fan is decorated with a *sumi-e* 墨絵 style painting of auspicious representations: a stork, pine branches, and clouds. The pine branches are colored golden brown, and the clouds are suggested by silvery brush strokes and faint gold speckles. This common type of "album fan" is made with plain paper so that one can clearly see written or sketched decoration (Salwey,

1894:62, 78). This type of fan sometimes is used as part of formal gifts, by placing it on top of boxes containing the objects presented. The Japanese consider the folding fan to be an emblem of life and, therefore, to be particularly appropriate as a gift on the occasion of a first meeting with a stranger. "The rivet-end is regarded as the starting-point, and as the rays of the fan expand so the life widens out towards a prosperous future" (Salwey, 1894:67; Miyoshi, 1979:50, for Japanese symbolic use of fans).

Remarks: This fan probably was an informal gift that Perry received at one of the several banquets held ashore or on board ship. Neither the American nor Japanese offical lists of "Japanese presents" includes folding fans, although there are frequent references to them in various private journals,

USNM ECC 280?

including S. Wells Williams' in which he lists the 24 folding fans given to him and others in the Ryūkyū (Hora, 1970:482). Perry received 10 folding fans at Naha on June 1853 (cf. Appendixes IIIA, IIIC). This fan was identified as a "paper fan" (1953-AL; 1859-ACB), and a "common fan" (ECC). This fan was exhibited at the Japan Society, New York City, in 1969.

Additional Specimens: ECC 111 and ECC 290a–d, all identical to ECC 290e.

48 Fan (*sensu; ōgi*)
USNM ECC 280?
L: 28.6 cm, W: 50 cm (top when unfolded)

Description: Folding fan made of paper and bamboo.
Characteristics: Black lacquered paper is pasted on the front and back sides of 27 flat bamboo ribs, which are framed and fastened at the base with a *kaname*. The fan face is decorated with the *sumi-e* style painting in silver of chrysanthemum blossoms and the leaves of iris and pine. The outer surface of the fan frame is colored black.

USNM ECC 290g

49   Fan (*sensu; ōgi*)
USNM ECC 290g
L: 28.6 cm, W: 46 cm (top when unfolded)

Description: White, folding fan made of bamboo and paper.

Characteristics: For standard materials used and method of construction see entry 47. Part of the fan face is light blue with patches of silver speckles. It is decorated with a *sumi-e* style painting of *tessen; tessenka* 鉄線花 (clematis) blossoms, leaves, and vines in silvery grey. Dark blue coloring is added on some flower petals. Both the front and back upper margins are edged in gold. *Tessenka,* although indigenous to China, appears frequently as the subject of paintings and poetry, especially during the Edo period (pers. comm. Hauge). This is a good example of an album fan with a plain face designed for a *sumi-e* style painting.

Remarks: This fan probably was one of the fans included in the Ryūkyūan official gifts (cf. Appendixes IIIA, IIIC) or an informal gift that Perry received from an unspecified source (cf. entry 47, for various identifications and uses). It was exhibited along with ECC 290f at the Japan Society, New York City, in 1969.

NMAH-DAF Dudley 59873-N-00110

50 Fan (*sensu; ōgi*)
NMAH-DAF Dudley 59873-N-00110
L: 28.6 cm, W: ~ 40 cm (top when unfolded)

Description: Folding bamboo and paper fan.

Characteristics: White *minogami* (cf. entry 26) is mounted on both the front and back sides of 10 flat bamboo ribs, which are fastened at the base with a steel rivet. Salwey (1894:30) attributes the use of *minogami* in fan-making to its durability and textured surface that accommodates painting and printing. The obverse is decorated with a *sumi-e* style painting of bamboo and Mount Fuji, and the upper margins on both sides are edged in gold. On the obverse an inscription in the hand of the collector, Thomas C. Dudley (Purser's clerk on Commodore Perry's flagship, the *Powhatan*), reads: "Yokohama April 7th 1854. Presented to me by Chief of the Japan Land Forces Lajanoske Mount Fuji Jamma [yama]." This is a good example of an album fan with a plain face designed for sketches or writing to commemorate special occasions (Salwey, 1894:62, 78, for discussion of Japanese uses of album fans especially with foreign visitors).

Remarks: The fan, a gift of E.M. Guilmette, a descendant of the collector, was received in 1977.

NMAH-DAF Dudley 59873-N-00111

51 Fan (*sensu; ōgi*)
NMAH-DAF Dudley 59873-N-00111
L: 28.6 cm, W: ~ 40 cm (top when unfolded)

Description: Folding bamboo and paper fan.

Characteristics: White *minogami* is mounted on both the front and back sides of 10 flat bamboo ribs, which are fastened at the base with a steel rivet or *kaname*. The upper margins are edged in gold, and a line-drawing portrait in black depicts Thomas C. Dudley, the collector, on obverse. An inscription in the hand of the collector at the upper left reads: "My portrait twice as natural, done by a Japanese; at Yokohama Jeddo [Edo] Bay, March 31, 1854." The reverse is blank. Undoubtedly, this was a personal gift to Dudley (Salwey, 1984:67, for Japanese symbolic use of fans, especially its appropriateness as a gift on the occasion of a first meeting with a stranger; for similar gift fans, cf. entries 47–49).

Remarks: The fan was a gift of E.M. Guilmette, a descendant of the collector; it was received in 1977.

USNM ECC 290f

52 Fan (*sensu; ōgi*)
USNM ECC 290f
L: 28.6 cm, W: 40 cm (top when unfolded)

Description: White, folding bamboo and paper fan.
Characteristics: The fan face is decorated with a *sumi-e* style painting in silvery grey of five cranes in flight. The clouds in the background are suggested by a mound-like semicircle behind the clouds. For fan-making materials and method, cf. entry 47.

Remarks: This probably was one of the 10 or 20 fans received at Naha in June 1853 (cf. Appendixes IIIA, IIIC) or an informal gift that Perry received ashore or on board ship. This fan and ECC 209g were exhibited at the Japan Society, New York City, in 1969.

USNM ECC 22 (obverse side)

53 Fan (*uchiwa* うちわ ; *dansen* 団扇)
USNM ECC 22
L: 34.3 cm, W: 29.5 cm

Description: Rounded rectangular picture fan made of paper pasted on a bamboo frame with a handle splayed to the top.

Characteristics: The fan-face is decorated with a woodcut color print of *ukiyo-e* painting in the style of *nishiki-e* 錦絵 (brocade pictures; the full color print) and is entitled "*Edo meisho mizu no omokage*" 江戸名所水のおもかげ (An image of water scene [from] famous views of Edo [series], [1849–1853] (see B.W. Robinson, 1961:30–32, for dating). The fan is signed by the artist, Hiroshige I 廣重 (1797–1858). The series, "Famous views of Edo" was designed specifically for fans (Suzuki, 1958:18). The scene includes three women at a river bank who are seated under wisteria blossoms and viewing the water. The fan has a predominantly blue color

USNM ECC 22 (reverse side)

design with additional colors of black and rose tint. Other inscriptions include the sub-title, "*Kameido*" 亀戸 (a scenic place on the bank of the *Sumida-gawa* 隅田川 (river)); *fuji-dana* 藤棚 (wisteria trellis); the seal of the censor "Muramatsu" in combination with *fuku;* and the publisher's trade mark "Sampei" 三平, in a fan-shape enclosure [of] Yokkaichi 四日市 (B.W. Robinson, 1961:30–32, 57–59; Lane, 1978:314–316, for *ukiyo-e* publishers' seals; Kurihara, 1901:186–192, for origins of family trade marks). The reverse

ornamentation, also with a blue and rose tint, depicts a moonlit night view of the river with watercraft at anchor, under the same title, by Shigenobu 重宜 (1787–1832) (Lane, 1978:324). Two additional inscriptions are the artist's signature with *hitsu* 筆 (written or painted by) and the publisher's trade mark, "Sampei."

Remarks: This probably was one of the 40 fans received at Edo Bay, 16 July 1853 (Williams, 1910:68, for listing of Japanese presents; Taylor, 1859:438, for descriptions).

USNM ECC 4 (obverse side)

54 Fan (uchiwa; dansen)
USNM ECC 4
L: 34.5 cm, W: 28.8 cm

Description: Rounded rectangular picture fan ornamented with a woodcut color print in the style of *nishiki-e*.

Characteristics: The print is entitled, "*Mizu no nagame*" 水のながめ (A shore view, or Water viewing). It was made no earlier than 1844 (see Strange, 1906:45–46, for dating) by Toyokuni III (also known as Kunisada I, 1786–1864), and it is signed Toyokuni *ga* 豊国画 (painted by Toyokuni.) The scene is a group portrait of a *samurai* in formal garb, wearing two swords and holding a fan, standing beside a young maiden and a woman, all of which is set against a waterscape with a group

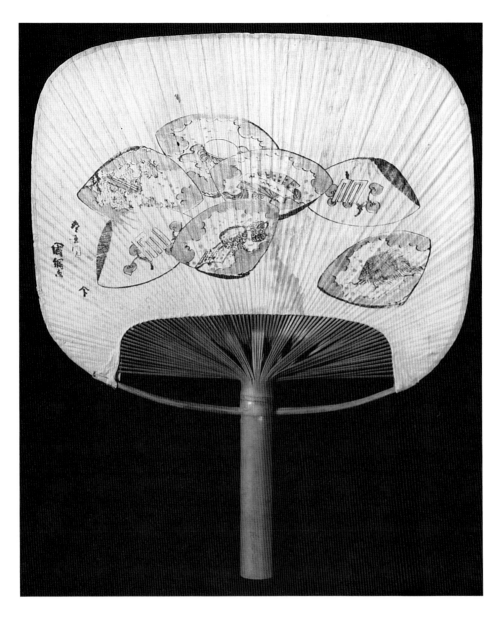

USNM ECC 4 (reverse side)

of onlookers in the background. The coloring is predominantly blue, with added tan and rose tints. The censors' seals are partially hidden and, therefore, undecipherable. The reverse is ornamented with a woodcut print in pink depicting seven shell halves used for *kai-awase* 貝合せ (shell-matching game), which in turn are decorated with such auspicious objects as a tortoise, a fan, a book, and lacquerware. The painting is by Kunitsuna 國綱 (1805–1868) (Roberts, 1976:98), and the publisher's trade mark reads: "Yenshu-ya Matabei, of Horiye-cho" (B.W. Robinson, 1961:57–59).

Remarks: This fan probably was one of the fans received at Edo Bay in July 1853 (Williams, 1910:68; Taylor, 1859:438). It was exhibited at the National Portrait Gallery, Washington, D.C., in 1977.

USNM ECC 5 (obverse side)

55 Fan (uchiwa; dansen)
USNM ECC 5
L: 34.6 cm, W: 29.4 cm

Description: Rounded rectangular picture fan made of paper.

Characteristics: The obverse ornamentation is a woodcut full-color *nishiki-e* print of a woman reading. It is entitled "*En'gyoku zoroi*" 艶曲揃 (Love verse, or Love story series) and was made ca. 1849–1853 (B.W. Robinson, 1961:30–33;

Lane, 1978:297, for identification of censors' seals and sample signatures for dating) by Utagawa Kuniyoshi 歌川国芳 (1798–1861) (Roberts, 1976:98). Additional decorations include a potted plant with peony blossoms and a crane design on the *kimono* fabric. The predominant color is indigo blue, with additional black, tan, and rose colors. Various inscriptions and seal marks include the artist's signature, Ichiyūsai Kuniyoshi *ga* 一勇齊国芳画 (painted by Ichiyūsai Kuniyoshi), with his personal *kiri* 桐 (paulownia) seal; *horitake* 彫竹 (engraving on bamboo); the censor's seal, *fuku* in combination with

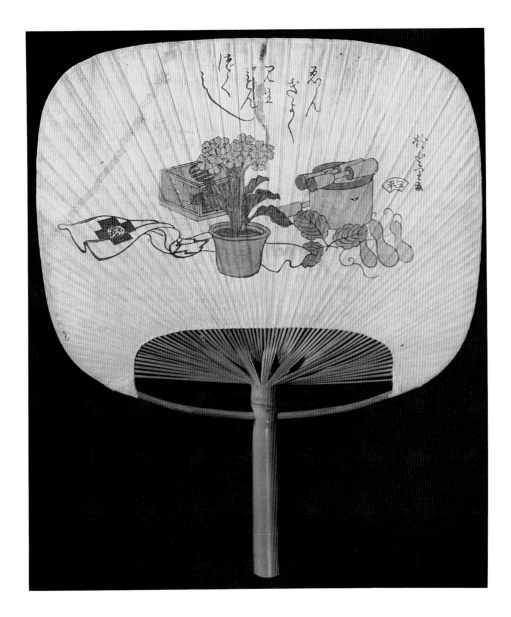

USNM ECC 5 (reverse side)

Muramatsu 村松 ; the printer's imprint "Sampei" ⟨平三⟩ in *senkei* 扇形 (fan-shape box); and the *aratame* 改 (examination) seal (examined in the second month of the year of the ox [1853]) (B.W. Robinson, 1961:31–33, for identification of *aratame* seals). A woodcut print of a still life in grey and rose colors decorates the reverse. Depicted are a potted blossoming plant, a box, gourds, a mortar with pestles, the printer's seal "Sampei," and the inscriptions: "*Oshri-e*" [?] 於当里画 (picture for the reverse [of the fan?]) and the title "*En'gyoku mitate hin* [?] *zukushi*" ゑんぎょく見立てひんづくし (Selected series of erotic objects [?]).

Remarks: This probably was one of the fans received in July 1853, at Edo Bay, via Kayama Eizaemon 香山栄左衛門, Assistant Magistrate of Uraga (Williams, 1910:68, journal entry for 16 July 1854; Taylor, 1859:438, for his description of the fans "covered with hideously distorted ... pictures of Japanese ladies"). The fan was exhibited at the Naval Historical Foundation's Truxtun Decatur Naval Museum, Washington, D.C., in 1975–1976, and also at the National Portrait Gallery, Washington, D.C., in 1977.

USNM ECC 25 (obverse side)

56 Fan (*uchiwa; dansen*)
USNM ECC 25
L: 34.6 cm, W: 29.4 cm

Description: Rounded rectangular picture fan made of paper.

Characteristics: The fan face is ornamented with a woodcut *nishiki-e* print of a party of men and women disembarking, and it is entitled "*Kazusa Kisarazu Bōsō*

meisho" 上総木更津房総名所 (A view at Kisarazu, Kazusa, Bōsō district [modern Chiba Prefecture] scenic views series). It was made ca. 1851–1853, by Hiroshige I 廣重 and is signed. Hiroshige made several visits to the Bōsō district between 1844–1852 (*USKH,* appendix: chronology). The view includes Mount Fuji in the distance, sailing boats afloat, and a *torii* 鳥居 (shrine gate) standing on shore among pine trees. The predominant color is indigo blue, with added tints of rose and tan. Other inscriptions are the censors' seal, "Watanabe

USNM ECC 25 (reverse side)

[Shoyemon] in combination with Mera [Taichiro]," and the publisher's trade mark, an ideograph for *tsuji* 辻 that is enclosed in a square, (?) "Tsujiya Yasubei, of Nandemma-cho" (B.W. Robinson, 1961:30–33, 58–59, for dating and identification of publisher). The reverse is decorated with a color print of "*Shōgatsu jibiki hatsuosame no zu*" 正月地引初納之図 (Painting of the New Year seine), also by Hiroshige, which depicts men and women at the shore pulling fishnet ropes. The scene is rendered in a blue-green and rose tint color design. Inscribed are the artist's signature and the identical trade mark as on the obverse of the fan.

Remarks: This fan probably was included in the first group of Japanese presents presented to Perry at Edo Bay in July 1853 (Williams, 1910:68, for his 16 July journal entry; Taylor, 1859:438, for his description of decorated Japanese fans).

USNM ECC 3 (obverse side)

57 Fan (*uchiwa; dansen*)
USNM ECC 3
L: 35.2 cm, W: 29.5 cm

Description: Rounded rectangular picture fan made of paper on a bamboo frame with a handle splayed to the top.

Characteristics: The obverse is ornamented with a wood-cut *nishiki-e* print of a bust of a woman. According to B.W. Robinson (1961:30–32), this signed fan by Ichiyūsai Ku-

niyoshi is entitled "*Sampuku-tsui*" 三婦久対 (Portrait of woman in triptych), and the date of the censors' seal is 1849. Lane (1978:298) states that the full title is "*Shogei-kurabe Sampuku tsui*" 諸芸位三婦久対 (Women of accomplishments in triptych) and gives the date as 1846. The rust- and brown-striped kimono pattern dominates the design, which is set against a backgound coloring of black, tan, and blue. Various inscriptions and symbols include the artist's personal seal of *kiri* (paulownia) crest (B.W. Robinson, 1961:15, 28);

USNM ECC 3 (reverse side)

the seal of censor Yoshimura in combination with "Kinugasa" (B.W. Robinson, 1961:30, 32); and the publisher's mark, "Sampei [of] Yokkaichi" [in modern Mie Prefecture] (B.W. Robinson, 1961:56–60). The reverse is decorated with a color print of a painting by Hiroshige II 廣重二世 (1829–1869). Depicted are a gourd, on which is inscribed a *waka* 和歌 (poem), and various seasonal floral representations. It is signed "Rissai" 立斎 or "Ryūsai" (Lane, 1978:229), which is Hiroshige's *gō* 号 (pseudonym) (Roberts, 1976:45; Strange, 1906:51, especially for reference to Kuniyoshi and Hiroshige II works on fan-shape color prints).

Remarks: This fan probably was one of the 40 fans received during Perry's first visit to Japan in July 1853 (Williams, 1910:68, for his 16 July 1853 entry; Taylor, 1859:438, for a description of the fans).

58 Umbrella (*kasa* 傘)
USNM ECC 426
L: 73 cm

Description: A man's common *amagasa* 雨傘 (rain umbrella) with *ja-no-me* 蛇の目 (lit. snake's eye) design construction.

Characteristics: The umbrella is made from a single piece of bamboo split into 52 ribs and covered with oil- and lacquer-finished paper. The ribs are gathered at the top to allow the umbrella to be opened and shut, and a bamboo handle is attached. An ochre decorative band, approximately 24.5 cm wide, circles the center of the deep blue umbrella canopy. The giving of umbrellas as official gifts may be of Chinese origin. In China, an elaborate umbrella sometimes is presented to a popular official when he or she leaves their district. It is considered to be a token of respect and purity and a symbol of dignity and high rank (Williams, 1976:413, for Chinese practice and symbolism).

Remarks: Various lists have entries for umbrellas: "*kasa*" in the AWL (*BGKM,* 1914, volume 6, page 201); 100 "*amagasa*" in the SGL (*BGKM,* 1914, volume 6, page 312); 10 "*konji ja-no-me gasa*" 紺地蛇の目傘 (deep blue umbrella of snake's eye design construction) received from Ido Tsushima-no-kami in the NGL (*BGKM,* 1912, volume 4, page 559); and 30 "*ja-no-me gasa*" included in the articles prepared for the Shimoda bazaar (*BGKM,* 1916, volume 8, page 553). Both the HNL and PJL note 20 umbrellas as gifts from Ido. This umbrella was entered in the 1859-ACB and 1953-AL as one of 57 identical "common umbrellas," ECC 389–556. The NGL's description of 10 umbrellas received from Ido approximates the deep blue colored *ja-no-me gasa* described above. This umbrella was exhibited at the Naval Historical Foundation's Truxtun Decatur Naval Museum in 1975–1976.

Additional Specimens: ECC 389–425, 427–445, all identical to ECC 426.

 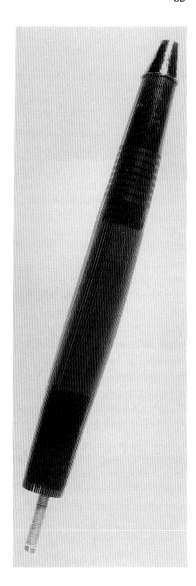

USNM ECC 426 (left, partially opened; right, closed)

59 Smoking pipes (*kiseru* 煙管)
USNM ECC 36–43
various sizes

Description: Tobacco pipes with straight *rao* 羅宇 (bamboo stems) of narrow diameter that range from 3 to 3.7 cm.

Characteristics: Fitted on one end of each pipe is an elongated brass *suikuchi* 吸口 (mouthpiece), and into the other end is a small *gankubi* 雁首 (lit. the long neck of flying geese), or pinch bowl, which is brazed at a right angle to the front-stem fitting. Japanese tobacco pipes originally were large and sometimes were carried over the shoulder and used as a weapon. A man's pipe is usually 6–8 inches (15.3–20.4 cm) in length, whereas a woman's often is longer, i.e., 1½ ft (37.1 cm) (Newman and Ryerson, 1964:116, for conventional pipe sizes). The type described above is a common variety. It usually is inserted into a pipe sheath that is then carried either by thrusting it under the girdle or, together with a pipe pouch, hung from the girdle by a cord and *netsuke* 根付 (an ornamental object for suspending a pouch or other objects worn above the girdle). The sheaths may be made of leather, papier-mâché, wood, ivory, or bone (Morse, 1917, volume 1, page 7; Boger, 1964:274–275, for pipe sheaths). The dimensions and descriptions of individual pipes are as follows. ECC 37 (L: 26.8 cm, D: 3 cm) has a pipe stem that is decorated with a stenciled *sayagata* 紗綾形 (continuous linked swastikas) pattern in *kiribori* 切彫 (perforated; dotted) design in black. Incised on the front-stem fitting is the pipe maker's signature, Kiyoharu 清合. ECC 36 (L: 25.0 cm, D: 3.5 cm) has a plain bamboo stem with a short mouthpiece and no ornamentation. ECC 38 (L: 25.0 cm, D: 3.0 cm) has a pipe stem decorated with a stencilled *kikkō* 亀甲 (tortoise-shell) pattern in *kiribori* design in black. ECC 39 (L: 24.5 cm, D: 3.7 cm) is partially decorated with ringed shallow grooves on the metal fittings of the front stem. ECC 40 (L: 25.4 cm, D: 3.0 cm) has a pipe stem that is decorated with a dark brown print of a figure of a woman standing under willow branches and a bird in flight. ECC 41 (L: 22.5 cm, D: 3.5 cm) has white brass fittings decorated with incised plum and peony blossoms. ECC 42 (L: 19.2 cm, D: 3.2 cm) has a short bamboo pipe stem with no ornamentation. ECC 43 (L: 18.8 cm, D: 3.2 cm) has a short pipe stem with an elongated (7 cm) mouthpiece. The metal fittings are white brass.

Remarks: These pipes were received at Naha in June 1853 and in July 1854 (cf. Appendixes IIIA, IIID). Two sample specimens (ECC 35, 40) were exhibited at the Japan Society, New York City, in 1969.

Additional Specimens: ECC 35 is identical to ECC 37.

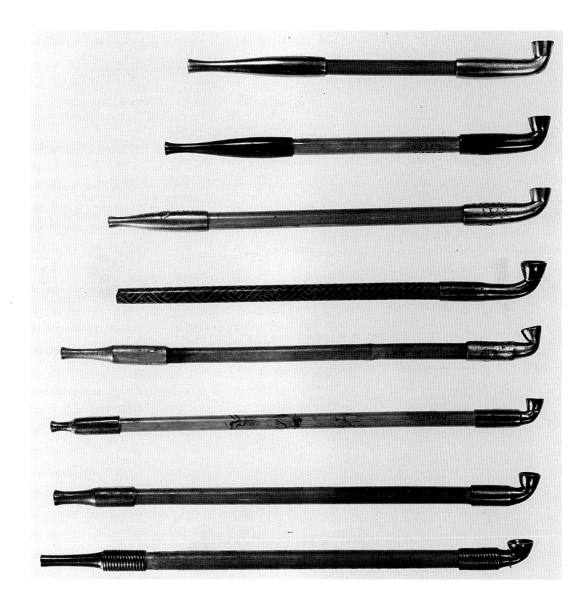

From top to bottom: USNM ECC 43, ECC 42, ECC 41, ECC 38, ECC 37, ECC 40, ECC 36, ECC 39

60 *"Peruri zō Kita-Amerika jimbutsu"* ペルリ像北亜墨
利加人物 **(Portrait of Perry, a North American)**
USNM ECC 398.566
L: 47.5 cm, W: 35.5 cm (inclusive of frame)

Description: Color woodblock print portrait of Perry, by
an anonymous Japanese artist in 1854.

Characteristics: An identical portrait is in the Paul Blum
private collection (1968-SIJE), and another is in the Kurofu-
nekan 黒船館 (Blackship Museum), located in Kashiwazaki
[city], Nagano prefecture, Japan.

Remarks: The portrait was reproduced in Morison
(1967:375) and also in *"Hajimete deatta Amerika"*
初めて出会った亜墨利加 (The First Encounter with
America), *Yokohama* ヨコハマ , special supplementary issue
(November 1978, page 9). It was included in "America's
Diplomacy," an exhibit held at the National Archives,
Washington, D.C., 15 April–1 August 1977. It was the gift of
Mrs. Lispenard S. Crocker, who acquired the print while her
husband, Edward Savage Crocker (1895–1968), served in the
United States diplomatic service. The museum received it in
1961.

USNM ECC 398.566

61 **"A village inn near Yeddo Japan"**
NMNH-NAA Art USNM 047292.00
L: 9 cm, W: 12 cm (exclusive of borders)

Description: Scene of a Japanese roadside village inn with
a group of travelers resting.

Characteristics: Included in the village scene is an open
kago 駕籠 (palanquin) made of split bamboo. The *kago*
bears a seat of woven bamboo wicker-work that is hung from a long
bamboo pole that rests on the shoulders of two carriers, one in
front, the other in back. Trees, shrubberies, and a partial view of
a bridge over a river also are included in the scene.

Remarks: The photograph, in sepia tone, is of a painting by
William Heine, ca. 1853–1854, who was the principal artist for
the Japan Expedition. The artist's signed inscription on the
reverse of the photo mount reads: "The illustrations in my work
are about four times this size." The caption also is in the artist's
handwriting.

MNHN-NA A Art USNM 047292.00

A village inn near Yeddo Japan.

The illustrations in my work are about four times
this size.
W. Heine

NMNH-NA A Art USNM 047292.00 (inscription on reverse of photo)

NMNH-NA A Art USNM 086443.00

NMNH-NA A Art USNM 086442.00

62 "Officer of Japan"
NMNH-NA A Art USNM 086443.00
L: 22 cm, W: 15 cm (exclusive of borders)

Description: Pencil sketch on paper of full-length front view of a Japanese military officer in formal dress.

Characteristics: The officer is wearing a *jingasa* 陣笠 (lacquered wooden helmet), an *haori* 羽織 (short loose jacket) with *mon* 紋 (family crest) marks, *hakama* 袴 (loose skirt-like trousers), *ama-geta* 雨下駄 (wooden clogs with deep cleats used for wet weather), and two swords. The work is by an anonymous artist, ca. 1853–1854. A handwritten caption on the front and an inscription in the same hand on the reverse of the mount reads: "Sketch made in Japan by a Naval Officer apparently with the Perry Ex[pedition]" and is signed "W.H." (Walter Hough, Curator, USNM, Division of Ethnology, 1908–1935).

Remarks: This sketch tentatively is attributed to William Heine, whose style of drawing in "Loo Choo Woman," entry 64, is similar to this drawing.

63 "Japanese Woman"
NMNH-NA A Art USNM 086442.00
L: 22.5 cm, W: 17.5 cm (exclusive of borders)

Description: Pencil sketch on paper of a full-length portrait of a Japanese woman.

Characteristics: The woman is shown wearing native semiformal attire of *kimono* 着物 worn with *haori, geta* (native footwear), and the Edo period hair-style with an ornamental *kushi* 櫛 (comb). The work is by an anonymous artist, ca. 1853–1854. The handwritten caption on the front and the inscription on the reverse of the mount are in the same hand. The inscription, "Sketch made in Japan by a Naval officer apparently with the Perry Ex[pedition]," is signed W.H. (Walter Hough).

Remarks: The sketch tentatively is attributed to William Heine.

NMNH-NA A Art USNM 086441.00

NMNH-NA A Art USNM 086444.00

64 "Loo Choo Woman"
NMNH-NA A Art USNM 086441.00
L: 24 cm, W: 14 cm (exclusive of borders)

Description: Full-length portrait of a Ryūkyūan woman in native costume.
Characteristics: The woman is carrying grass-like material. Especially notable is the hair arrangement with an ornamental hair-pin.
Remarks: The unsigned pencil drawing on paper is by William Heine (1817–1885), ca. 1853–1854, Naha, Ryūkyū. Heine was the principal artist with Perry's Japan Expedition, 1853–1854. The attribution is based on comparison of the handwritten caption on the front of this sketch with Heine's signed inscription on reverse of the mount of the photograph, "A village inn near Yeddo Japan," entry 61.

65 "Japanese Soldier"
NMNH-NA A Art USNM 086444.00
L: 24 cm, W: 14 cm (exclusive of borders)

Description: Full-length sideview of *samurai*, sketched in pencil on paper.
Characteristics: The *samurai* is in travelling attire, with two swords, leggings, and special footwear called *zōri* 草履 (straw sandals). The work is by an anonymous artist in Japan, ca. 1853–1854. The handwritten caption on the front and the inscription on the reverse of the mount are in the same hand. The inscription, "Sketch made in Japan by a Naval Officer apparently with the Perry Ex[pedition]," is signed W.H. (Walter Hough).
Remarks: The sketch possibly is by William Heine, the principal artist of the Japan Expedition, whose style of drawing in "Loo Choo Woman," entry 64, is similar to this sketch.

NMNH-NAA Art USNM 086445.00

NMAH-DAF Dudley 59873-N-0084

66 "Aino of Yezo"

NMNH-NAA Art USNM 086445.00
L: 25 cm, W: 15.5 cm (exclusive of borders)

Description: Watercolor painting on paper of two Ainu males.

Characteristics: The full-length figures are barefooted and are wearing knee-length *atsushi* 厚子 (bark-cloth) robes. Especially notable are the length of their hair and their full beards. The painting is executed in predominantly dark blue coloring with additional light brown and beige tints. The work is by an anonymous artist, ca. 1854, Hakodate, Hokkaido. The handwritten caption on the front and the inscription on reverse of the mount is in the same hand. The inscription, "Sketch made in Japan by a Naval Officer apparently with the Perry Ex[pedition]," is signed W.H. (Walter Hough).

67 Sketch (*shaseiga* 写生画)

NMAH-DAF Dudley 59873-N-0084
L: 18.5 cm, W: 18.1 cm

Description: Hand-colored, pencil sketch of a standing group of Ryūkyūan officials in native dress.

Characteristics: The sketch is signed by T.C. Dudley, and the caption, in the hand of the artist, reads: "Nagadore [Nagadō 長堂] and Itsisi [Itarajiki 板良敷] Napa Kiang—Loo Choo—July 1854." Itarajiki was the interpreter for the Ryūkyūan regent, Shō Kō-kun 尚広勲 (Hora, 1970:81). The interpreter's name is variously rendered as Ichirazichi (Hawks, 1856:219, 247), Adjirashi (Williams, 1910:13), and Idjirashi (Williams, 1910:14) (Hora, 1970:37). Napa Kiang is the present-day city of Naha. Dudley apparently mistook the place name Nagadō as the name of a Ryūkyūan official. Lewis (in Graff, 1952:98) identified Napa Kiang as a town; however, Preble refered to it in his diary as the Napa River (Szczesniak, 1962:28).

Remarks: The sketch, received by the museum in 1977, was a gift of E.M. Guilmette, a descendant of the collector.

NMAH-DAF Dudley 59873-N-0082

68 Pictorial map (*ezu* 絵図)
NMAH-DAF Dudley 59873-N-0082
L: 40.6 cm, W: 61.5 cm

Description: Black and white *han'ga* 版画 (woodblock print) map of Edo Bay, depicting Perry's arrival in 1853, entitled "*Kaei kaisei taihei anmin kan*" 嘉永改正泰平安民鑑 (lit. A view or mirror of the land in peace and tranquility, revised edition of Kaei period [1848–1853]).

Characteristics: The names of Toda Izu-no-kami 戸田伊豆守 (Lord of the Izu district (modern Shizuoka prefecture)) and Izawa Mimasaka-no-kami 伊沢美作守 (Lord of the Mimasaka district (modern Okayama prefecture)) are printed underneath the name of Uraga *go-bugyō* 浦賀御奉行 (the honorable chief magistrate of Uraga). The map depicts the Japanese harbor defense units, including the names of respective *daimyō* 大名 (lord), the names of the *han* 藩 (fief) that they ruled, the *mon* (family crest), and their annual rice stipends in *koku* 石 (measure of capacity; 1 *koku* equals 180 liters or 4.96 bushels), with a view of Perry's ships assembled in the bay.

Remarks: The print was a gift from E.M. Guilmette, a descendant of the collector; it was received in 1977.

NMNH-NA A MS7145

69 Pictorial map (*ezu*)

NMNH-NA A MS7145

L: 48 cm, W: 69 cm

Description: Black and white woodblock print pictorial map of Edo Bay, depicting Perry's arrival in 1853.

Characteristics: One section illustrates a scene of Commodore Perry, his principal aide, Commander Adams, and their entourage during the landing at Kurihama 久里浜. Additional illustrations include two ship portraits with their respective dimensions, number of crew, and other observations; a list of *han;* the names of the *daimyō* and their crests; and the number of men each lord had assigned to the harbor defense units.

Added to the list are the Uraga chief magistrates, Toda Izu-no-kami and Izawa Mimasaka-no-kami, together with some members of the reception committee and *Bakufu* 幕府 (central government) inspectors.

Remarks: This print was included in an exhibit entitled "Around the World," held at the Historic Warner House, Portsmouth, New Hampshire, 31 July–5 August 1939 (ECC). English labels are affixed on the borders of the mounting. The map was received by the museum in 1961 as a gift of Mrs. Lispenard S. Crocker. In 1984, it was transferred from the Department of Anthropology, ethnography collection, to the National Anthropological Archives.

Bamboo, Wood, Straw, and Fiber Products

70 Bamboo bottle (*take-sasae* 竹小筒)
USNM ECC 165
H: 18.2 cm, D: 5.5 cm

Description: Portable container, *take-sasae* (lit. small bamboo tube), made of a cylindrical section of bamboo that is closed with an unpunctuated node at the base and a wooden disk cover fitted at the top.

Characteristics: Bamboo bottles such as this were used for carrying wine for traveling or picnics (*NKDJ*, 1976, volume 13, page 6; Holme, 1892:33, for varied uses). The disk cover is pierced on one side by a small, straw-like tube with stopper. On the opposite side, there is a small air hole. Another small bamboo tube pierces the upper part of the container through which is threaded a thin, black carrying cord that is joined to a similar, shorter cord attached to the stopper.

Remarks: The bottle was received from Izawa Mimasaka-no-kami and probably was one of the articles included in "*take zaiku-rui shina-jina*" 竹細工類品々 (various bamboo ware) (Hora, 1970:242). The HNL identifies part of Izawa's gifts as "1 box bamboo woven articles" (cf. Appendix I). The AWL includes bamboo ware (*BGKM*, volume 6, page 201). This item was entered as a "bamboo water canteen" in both the 1859-ACB and the 1953-AL. In the ECC it was listed as a "*suitō*" 水筒 (water canteen). The bottle was exhibited at the Truxtun Decatur Naval Museum, Washington, D.C., in 1975–1976.

Additional Specimens: Two other specimens, ECC 165 and 9209, are identical to ECC 164.

USNM ECC 165

USNM ECC 279

71 Back scratcher (*mago-no-te* 孫の手)
USNM ECC 279
L: 35 cm, W: 1.8 cm

Description: Mago-no-te (lit. the hand of grandchild) made of a long, thin bamboo strip.

Characteristics: The end of the back scratcher is slightly curved and widened forming a hand-like shape, the end of which is cut irregularly to create sharp edges. The design is to provide, when used, the sensation of nail scratches.

Remarks: It probably was one of the items included in the bamboo woven articles received from Izawa Mimasaka-no-kami.

Additional Specimens: ECC 279 includes 6 additional specimens, each of slightly different size.

USNM ECC 277, 278

72 Massage rollers (*amma-ki* 按摩器)
USNM ECC 277, 278
H: 5 cm, L: 5.1 cm

Description: Wooden *amma-ki* (lit. implement for massaging human body), constructed from a partial section of bamboo cylinder with bevelled edges.

Characteristics: Mounted inside crosswise is a bar that pierces through a wooden ball-like disk, which is designed to revolve when pressed as a roller. Only the surface of the curved bamboo holder, fashioned so as to fit into the palm of one's hand, is stained dark. The construction is similar to a kneader called *hitori-amma* 独り按摩 (self shampooer) (Holme, 1892:39–40, for the user's posture and the effectiveness of the bamboo kneader).

Remarks: Probably these were articles that were included in the assorted bamboo ware received from Izawa Mimasaki-no-kami. These two rollers were exhibited at the Japan Society, New York City, in 1969. In 1969, Tsuji Yutaka, a newspaper correspondent for the *Asahi Shimbun,* Tokyo, was able to provide the Japanese term *amma-ki* for the objects.

Additional Specimens: ECC 277 has two additional specimens, one of which is only a fragment. ECC 278 also has two additional specimens. All the specimens are identical.

USNM ECC 314(a–g)

73 Writing brush (*fude* 筆)
USNM ECC 314(a–g)
L: 20 cm (average)

Description: A tuft of rabbit hair bound together and inserted in a narrow bamboo tube, the handle.

Characteristics: ECC 314 applies to six writing brushes with slight size variations; the letters a–g are arbitrary additons. Individual charateristics are as follows.

ECC 314a has a tapered brush tip that is covered by a bamboo tube. The slip of rice paper pasted on the handle is inscribed with the ideograph for "*kosui*" 湖水 (lit. lake water), which presumably is the maker's pseudonym.

ECC 314b has the same construction as ECC 314a. The light brown brush probably is made of badger's hair. It is shorter and thinner than ECC 314a; there is no inscription. A split in the brush cover is evident.

ECC 314c has the same construction as ECC 314a. This brush is thicker than ECC 314a and 314b and has a less-tapered brush top. The cover is missing, and a hole has been pierced through the midsection of the handle.

ECC 314d has the same construction as ECC 314a. The brush and the upper part of the handle are stained with a Western variety of ink.

ECC 314e is identical to ECC 314d.

ECC 314f has only the bamboo handle and brush cover remaining; the brush is missing. Incised on the handle in blue are three illegible ideographs; an ideograph in red reads "*fukki*" 復記 .

ECC 314g has only the bamboo handle and brush cover remaining; the brush is missing.

USNM ECC 166

74 Brush holder (*fude-tate* 筆立て)
USNM ECC 166
L: 14.5 cm, D: 9.5 cm

Description: Cylindrical open section of bamboo in natural color, which is mounted on an octagonal, light brown wooden base.

Characteristics: Receptacles such as this commonly are found on writers' tables where they are used to store brushes, knives, and other writing implements. Holme (1892:37) prefers the term "brush stand" to brush holder. The interior is lined with cream colored silk, whereas its exterior is decorated with a pair of incised figures of *minogame* with light and dark painted shading. The *minogame* figures are widely spaced; one is at the left bottom and the other to the upper right of an incised

red circle that surrounds the inscribed character "*furō*" 不老 (eternal youth; immortality), which is also in red.

Remarks: This definitely is one of the articles included in the assorted bamboo wares received from Izawa, as is indicated in the HNL. It was identified as a "bamboo goblet" in both the 1859-ACB and 1953-AL and was exhibited at the Japan Society, New York City, in 1969.

75 Basket (*kago* 籠)
USNM ECC 109
H: 8.5 cm, D: 29 cm

Description: Round, shallow fruit basket in light brown, made of thin *suzutake* 篠竹 or *sasa* 笹 (dwarf bamboo grass), with interlaced, open-work design.

Characteristics: The mouth of the basket is scalloped by bending the bamboo stems toward the base where they are twined. The *susudake* 煤竹 (smoked bamboo) effect of the silky textured brown coloring traditionally is obtained by storing clumps of bamboo high in farmhouse rafters for prolonged periods of time, thus exposing them to smoke and soot from the family hearth (*JI*, 1962:88, for coloring method).

Remarks: This basket was one of the woven bamboo articles either received from Izawa (HNL entry for "1 box bamboo woven articles"; cf. Appendix I) or purchased at Shimoda. "*Kudamono-ire maru kago*" 菓物入丸籠 (round fruit basket) of various sizes are included in the SML, the list of articles collected as additional gifts or for the several bazaars held at Shimoda during May and June 1854 (*BGKM*, volume 8, pages 543–544) in response to the AWL, which included "*kago zaiku mono*" 籠細工物 (basketry work) (cf. Appendix V).

76 Basket (*kago*)
USNM ECC 117
H: 4.5 cm, W: 4.5 cm, L: 30 cm

Description: Rounded rectangular, shallow fish basket.

Characteristics: The basket has an open-work design, with a high loop handle. It is made of brown-colored dwarf bamboo (cf. entry 75 for information about the weave and the process of brown coloring).

Remarks: This is one of the bamboo woven articles either received from Izawa (HNL) or purchased at Shimoda. Entries for "*sakana kago*" 肴籠 (fish basket) and "*naga kago*" 長籠 (long or rectangular basket) of various sizes are included in the SML (*BGKM*, 1916, volume 8, pages 542–543; cf. Appendix V).

Additional Specimens: A second basket (not illustrated), also numbered ECC 117, is a round fruit basket (H: 9 cm) with a missing loop handle. It too has an open-work design made of brown-colored (smoked) dwarf bamboo grass.

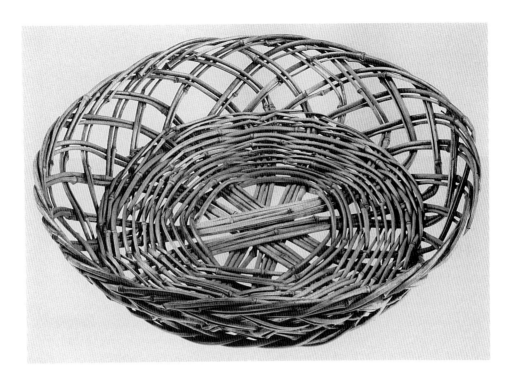

USNM ECC 109

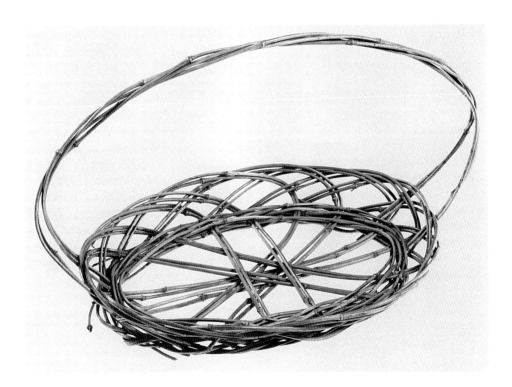

USNM ECC 117

USNM ECC 302

77 Family Shinto altar (*kamidana* 神棚)
USNM ECC 302
L: 58.4 cm, W: 20.3 cm, H: 37.5 cm

Description: Rectangular, wooden *kamidana* (lit. God's shelf) for household use.

Characteristics: The altar is a modified architectural reproduction of a Shinto shrine in traditional style, which is designed to be displayed upon a shelf. *Kamidana* are used as places of worship of Shintoist deities or for the safekeeping of charms, amulets, and other sacred objects. Three compartments with doors are fitted within the box-like structure. The center chamber, the sanctuary, contains a carved wooden figure of Daikoku 大黒 , the god of wealth, one of the seven gods of good fortune in the Japanese folk tradition derived from Brahmanism, Buddhism, Taoism, and Shintoism (Gunsaulus, 1922:12). Daikoku, who is worshipped as the special patron of farmers, stands on two rice bales while holding what is believed to be a magic hammer with which he can produce anything the human heart desires. He carries a large sack of treasures over his shoulder (Piggott, 1969:58–59; *CCJWA*, 1883:12; Shugio, 1896:351). Latticework ornaments the left and right front panels, and round, brass nail heads encircled with scalloped, black wooden disks are used to fasten the framework. Additional ornamentation consists of a low relief sculpture in wood of a modified heart-shape *inome kegyo* 猪目懸魚 (lit. wild boar's eye design gableboard decoration). *Kegyo* or *kengyo* (lit. suspended fish) is an architectural term for such decorations on a gableboard or bargeboard (pers. comm. Okada, conversation, March 1979). Over time, the *kegyo* fish-shape design on the altar has been lost, but the heart-shape decoration and the belief that it guards the building against fire have survived (*NKDJ*, 1976, volume 7, page 162).

Remarks: The altar was purchased by Dr. James Morrow, the scientist attached to Perry's expedition party, at Shimoda, June 1854 (Morrow in Cole, 1947:233; cf. Appendix IV).

USNM ECC 303

78 Family Shinto altar (*kamidana*)
USNM ECC 303
L: 34.2 cm, W: 16 cm, H: 35.2 cm

Description: Wooden household Shinto altar.

Characteristics: The altar is a modified reproduction of a Shinto shrine in the *kasuga* 春日 architectural style. The upright, box-like structure, with doors in front and concave roof surfaces, is set on a rectangular platform. A low relief of a heart-shape *inome kegyo* (cf. entry 77 for symbolism) decorates the gableboard. A wooden figure of Daikoku, the god of wealth (cf. entry 77 for full description), is placed inside the box, the sanctuary.

Remarks: The altar was purchased at Shimoda, June 1854, by Dr. James Morrow (Morrow in Cole, 1947:233; cf. Appendix IV). It was exhibited in Washington, D.C., at the Renwick Gallery of Art exhibition, "Celebration: A World of Art and Ritual," 17 March 1981– 26 June 1983.

USNM ECC 301

79 Family Shinto altar (*kamidana*)
USNM ECC 301
L: 101.5 cm, W: 41.3 cm, H: 50.8 cm

Description: Miniature wooden *kamidana* for household use.

Characteristics: This altar is a modified architectural reproduction done in the traditional style of the Hie 日吉 shrine (Boger, 1964:157–158, for illustrations of various shrine architectural styles) and designed for placement upon a shelf. *Kamidana* are used as places of worship of Shintoist dieties or for safekeeping of such objects as charms, amulets, and other objects of a religious nature (Morse, 1886:224–225, for an assortment of displayed objects). Five compartments with doors are fitted within the rectangular box-like structure. Grill work and an openwork design of stylized pine tree branches, cranes, and *kajiba* 梶葉 (oak leaves) ornament the structure. The pine and crane are symbols of longevity and happiness. Edmunds (1934:317) traces the pine and crane combination to Taoist origins, but notes that it is a common Japanese motif. The oak leaf symbol is associated with

offerings to the gods because of its use as a wrapper for certain dishes, whereas oak trees themselves are considered to be shrine guardians (Dower, 1971:65, for symbolic origins and associations). Additional ornamentation for the upper front of the structure is a low relief sculpture in wood of a modified heart-shape *inome kegyo* (cf. entry 77 for symbolism). A wooden figure of Ebisu 恵比寿, the god of fishermen and tradesmen, one of the seven gods of good fortune in Japanese folk tradition, stands in the central chamber. The Ebisu figure carries a fishing rod and a large *tai* 鯛 (sea-bream). Two carved wooden figures of *kara-shishi* 唐獅子 (lit. Chinese lion), act as guardian animals and flank the offering tray, *ozen* 御膳, at the entrance to the sanctuary.

Remarks: The altar was identified as a "household shrine" by the expedition scientist and collector, Dr. James Morrow, who purchased it at Shimoda in June 1854 (Morrow in Cole, 1947:233; cf. Appendix IV), and it is so entered in the 1859-ACB and 1953-AL. The ECC includes descriptions of the animal guardians as "two grotesque heads," the carved Ebisu figure as the "god of sustenance and fish market," and the word "Shinto."

NMAH-DAF Dudley 59873-N-0032 (with drawer closed)

80 Small box (*kobako* 小箱 ; *tebako* 手箱)
NMAH-DAF Dudley 59873-N-0032
L: 8.3 cm, W: 8.3 cm, H: 4.5 cm

Description: Small or handy box made of *hinoki* 檜
(Japanese cypress) wood with *mokuga* 木画 (lit. wood
picture; mosaic work on wooden objects) or *zōgan* 象眼
(inlay) decoration.

Characteristics: The four sides of the box are hollowed
out, and into one side is inserted a drawer-like construction that
slides. The side panels for the three sides apparently are
missing. The box top ornamentation consists of inlays of light
and dark brown natural wood pieces in geometric patterns,
including a pentacle, squares, and other shapes. It has been
identified (pers. comm. Tanabe) as a good example of the
woodcrafts produced in the Hakone 箱根 (Kanagawa prefecture) area, which is popularly known as Hakone *zaiku*
箱根細工 (Hakone handicrafts). The *mokuga* method of
decoration is said to have originated in the Nara period (AD
645–794), and various other materials such as ivory, horn, and
shell frequently are used (Sadaharu, 1968:104; Okada,

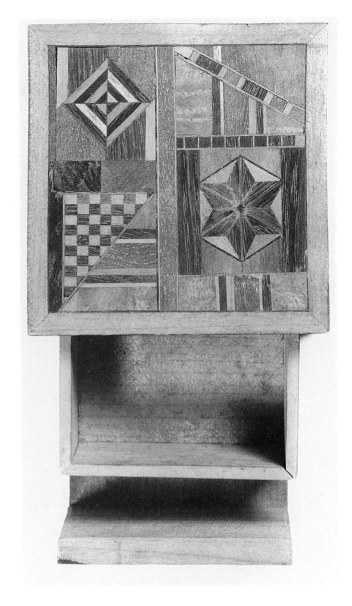

NMAH-DAF Dudley 59873-N-0032 (with drawer open)

1956:57–59, for various methods and types of woodcrafts
featuring *mokuga* decoration).

Remarks: This box probably was purchased at one of the
several bazaars held in both Hakodate and Shimoda. It was a
gift of E.M. Guilmette, a descendant of the collector and was
received in 1977.

MAH-DAF Dudley 59873-N-00136–37 (top view)

MAH-DAF Dudley 59873-N-00136–37 (side view)

81 Wooden clogs (*koma-geta* 駒下駄)
MAH-DAF Dudley 59873-N-00136-37
L: 17.7 cm, W: 7 cm, H: 7 cm

Description: A pair of common, oblong, women's foot-wear for everyday use, carved from a solid block of paulownia wood (Janata, 1965, entry 831; Morse, 1917, volume 1, page 3, for similar specimens).

Characteristics: Plaited rush insoles are fastened to the wooden base with iron tacks. White leather thongs pass through a hole in the front end of the sole and are fastened midway back at both sides. The holes are situated so that the thong fits comfortably between the first and second toes. *Koma-geta* made for use by men generally are called *nomeri-geta* のめり下駄, and one with a plaited rush sole is called *omote*

tsuki nomeri 表つきのめり (Endō, 1971, entry 227, for term and illustration). A similar type of *koma-geta,* particularly with iron tacks but with its height ranging from approximately 6 to 8 cm, is known as *Dōjima-geta,* 堂島下駄 which are used exclusively by traveling Edo prostitutes. The term is said to have originated in the Dōjima district, a well-established Osaka area (*NKDJ*, 1976, volume 14, pages 464–465). *Geta* are worn with or without *tabi* 足袋 (lit. foot-bag; ankle-length socks), which also have separate divisions for the big toe.

Remarks: The tag attached to the clogs states that they were the "first purchase in Japan by the Americans." The tag probably was written by the collector. This was a gift of E.M. Guilmette, a descendant of the collector; it was received in 1977.

USNM ECC 309

82 Straw raincoat (*mino* 蓑)
USNM ECC 449 (not illustrated)
L: 105 cm, W: 38 cm (at top)

Description: Rain gear made of overlapping layers of wide strands of *kasasuge* カサスゲ (*Carex dispalata*) type straw (pers. comm. Tanabe, conversation, July 1979) that flare out and taper toward the rear end.

Characteristics: Two strings are interwoven into the upper portion of the *mino*. When worn, they are to be tied in front. This style of raincoat commonly is known as a farmers' or peasants' raincoat, but its use is not limited to them. Variations in style exist (Janata, 1965, entries 278–280, for similar and other types; Tanaka, 1970, entry 27, for the type produced and used in Iwate prefecture; Yanagi, 1960, entry 45, for a northern variety produced in Aomori prefecture). In addition to straw, other materials, such as miscanthus, sedge, and hemp-palm, also are used (*NKDJ,* 1976, volume 18, page 634).

Remarks: Two pieces are cataloged under ECC 449. They were incorrectly identified as "grass skirts" in the 1859-ACB and ECC; the latter has the following notation: "Though these look like grass skirts, the very small waist may mean they were for some other purposes, probably raincoats." They were not included in the 1953-AL. They probably were purchased at Shimoda in June 1854. A SML entry reads: "Kaga *mino*" 加賀蓑 (straw raincoat from the province of Kaga [modern Ishikawa prefecture] (*BGKM,* 1916, volume 8, page 549). Photos are not available as the objects are too fragile to handle.

83 Broom (*hōki* 箒)
USNM ECC 309
L: 65 cm, W: 25 cm

Description: Broom made of corn stalks or *morokoshi-bōki* 箒 (Janata, 1965, entry 408, for identical specimen) for both indoor and outdoor use.

Characteristics: A sheaf of thin corn stalks is bound with an *akebi* アケビ (vine) (pers. comm. Tanabe, conversation, July 1979) to form a handle approximately 27 cm in length. The fine branches that spread out below the handle are cut at an angle to fit the floor or ground surface. The broom is not designed to be held vertically (specific features of Japanese brooms are noted in Morse, 1917, volume 1, page 147).

Remarks: The broom probably was a purchased item or an informal gift as it is not included in any of the available lists of Japanese presents.

USNM ECC 308

84 Broom (*hōki*)
USNM ECC 308
L: 77 cm, W: 22 cm

Description: Broom made of dark brown fibers of *shuro* 棕櫚, the hemp-palm (*Trachycarpus excelsus*) or *shuro-bōki* 棕櫚箒 (Janata, 1965, entry 407, for a similar specimen identified as a broom made of a species of palm, *Chamaerops excelsa*).

Characteristics: A wide and flat broom head with a straight edge is bound on a short bamboo handle (36.5 cm in length). It is designed exclusively for indoor use.

Remarks: This specimen is one of the 30 brooms given by Ido Tsushima-no-kami. An entry, "*shuro-bōki sanjuppon*" 棕櫚箒三拾本   (thirty hemp-palm brooms), is recorded in the NGL (*BGKM,* 1912, volume 4, page 556). An HNL entry accounts for "one box 30 coir brooms." It was identified as a "cocoanut broom" in the ECC.

Additional Specimens: ECC 307 has a shorter and thicker handle.

85 Hemp-palm fiber (*shuro-ge* 棕櫚毛)
USNM ECC 317 (not illustrated)
L: 51 cm, W: 19 cm

Description: A triangular sample of bark of the *shuro* plant with one end shredded, showing its coarse fiber in its natural dark brown color.

Characteristics: This piece probably was included in the box containing 30 brooms made of *shuro* fiber (cf. entry 84) in order to provide information about the raw material used. The *shuro* fiber is used for manufacturing other varied objects, such as hats, ropes, fish nets, and scrubbing brushes (*NKDJ,* 1976, volume 10, page 407).

Remarks: The label attached to the specimen incorrectly identifies it to be "cocoa nut fibre," and the error is reflected in the ECC.

Metalware

86 Egg cooking pan (*tamago-yaki* 卵焼)
USNM ECC 287
Pan, L: 12.3 cm, W: 12.3 cm, H: 2.3 cm
Handle, L: 9 cm, D: 2 cm

Description: Square, shallow, copper-plated tin pan, with short, hollow handle, used for cooking an omelet-like egg dish called "*tamago-yaki*," a term also applied to the cooking utensil itself (pers. comm. Tanabe, conversation, June 1979; *NKDJ*, 1976, volume 13, page 181).

Characteristics: The handle is pierced to accommodate a lanyard for hanging when not in use. When in use, an extra wooden handle (missing) is inserted into the metal handle for ease in handling (pers. comm. Tanabe, conversation, June 1979). The remaining legible inscriptions read: "Tazaka 田坂 [either a personal or place name] *yonsun* 四寸 [4 (Japanese) inches, which is ~12 cm; thus the pan size is 12 × 12 cm) *gojūgo ban*" 五拾五番 [number 55].

Remarks: The pan was incorrectly identified as "stew-pan" in the 1859-ACB, 1953-AL, and ECC. It probably was purchased by Dr. James Morrow at Shimoda in June 1854 (cf. Appendix IV for ML entry: "Specimens copper ware & plate"). The pan was exhibited at the Japan Society, New York City, in 1969.

USNM ECC 287

87 Iron pot (*kama* 釜)
USNM ECC 281
H: 20.3 cm, D: 31 cm

Description: Cast iron, globular cooking pot.

Characteristics: The pot has a wide flange (3.8 cm in diameter) around the middle of the body, and ring handles attached on each side near the mouth. The flange is intended to fit into a specially designed *ro* 炉 (hearth) or *kamado* 竈 (kitchen-range) for both indoor and outdoor use.

Remarks: This item was purchased by Dr. James Morrow at Shimoda during May–June 1854 (cf. Appendix IV for ML entry: "Iron pot'). It was entered as a "cast iron dinner pot" in both the 1859-ACB and the 1953-AL and as a "cast iron dinner pot or brazier" in the ECC. It was exhibited at the Japan Society, New York City, in 1969.

USNM ECC 281

USNM ECC 283

USNM ECC 332

88 Iron tea kettle (*teppin* 鉄瓶 ; *tetsubin* 鉄瓶 ; *tedori-gama* 手取り釜)
USNM ECC 283
H: 13.2 cm, D: 17.5 cm

Description: *Shibuichi* 四分一 (silver inlaid) cast iron kettle for use in the tea ceremony.

Characteristics: The globular-shape body with side spout is modified into an olpe-like vessel that tapers to a foot that forms a double curve. The handle loop and thin, flat cover are in brass. Attached to the cover is a small green bead handle. The main circular body is ornamented with the *shibuichi* effect of grey patina (Boger, 1964:93, 216–217, for *shibuichi* type metalware) in a relief design of the maple leaf. The foot, with a stylized, geometric wave pattern, also is in relief.

Remarks: Probably this was an item that was purchased or given informally, as none of the official lists of Japanese presents includes it. The AWL included iron and other metal wares (*BGKM,* 1914, volume 6, page 198). It was exhibited at the Japan Society, New York City, in 1969.

89 Iron wine server with stand (*chōshi* 銚子 , *gotoku* 五徳)
USNM ECC 332
Server, H: 8 cm, D: 14 cm
Stand, H: 7 cm, D: 11.2 cm

Description: Cast iron wine server (identification, pers. comm. Tanabe, conversation, June 1979) in a modified globular shape, with a side spout and a hollow, brass, loop handle.

Characteristics: The cover is missing. The body ornamentation is a grain pattern in high relief. The iron *gotoku* (kettle-holder) has hook-like pronged feet shaped into an elongated tripod, which is intended to fit into a brazier. It is a specially designed kettle for both warming and serving wine.

Remarks: The piece has been variously identified as an "iron bucket or teapot" in the 1859-ACB; "iron holders" in the 1953-AL; and as a "tea kettle" in the ML (cf. Appendix IV). It probably was purchased at Shimoda in June 1854.

USNM ECC 284

90 Iron wine server (*chōshi*) and stand (*gotoku*)
USNM ECC 284
Server, H: 8.8 cm, D: 13.5 cm
Stand, H: 8 cm, D: 13.5 cm

Description: Cast alloy of iron and silver, cylindrical kettle with a side spout and loop handle.

Characteristics: The body has the *shibuichi* effect of grey patina. The body ornamentation is a *nanten* (nandin) design in relief of berries and leaves, whereas pine branches and cherry blossoms decorate the iron handle. The iron *gotoku* (kettle holder or kettle stand) has hook-like pronged feet shaped into an elongated tripod, which is intended to fit into a specially designed brazier. The cover is missing.

Remarks: The piece probably was purchased by Dr. James Morrow at Hakodate in May 1854 (cf. Appendix IV for ML entry: "Large Iron Kettle"). This wine server is larger than the kettle (wine server) purchased at Shimoda (cf. entry 88). It was exhibited at the Japan Society, New York City, in 1969.

USNM ECC 284 (detail of handle)

USNM ECC 150

91   Sacred mirror (*shinkyō* 神鏡)
USNM ECC 150
D: 15.0 cm

Description: Round, copper, sacred mirror.
Characteristics: The surface of the mirror is ornamented with a pattern of closely set grain in low relief. The vertical inscription in the center reads: *"Aki-no-kuni Sunada-gōri Gion no yashiro shinkyō"* 安芸国沼田郡祇園社神鏡 (the sacred mirror from the Gion temple at Sunada district in the province of Aki [modern Hiroshima 広島 prefecture]) (see Wakayama, 1967:560, for Edo period administrative divisions; Papinot, 1948:118, for history of the mirror's religious affiliation). The sacredness of the mirror originates from the *yata-no-kagami* 八咫鏡 (synonymous with *shinkyō*), one of

the three Imperial treasures that are in the Ise jingū 伊勢神宮 (Ise Shinto shrine). The *yata-no-kagami* is closely related to the Japanese creation myth, and the original is said to have been in the form of a flower with eight petals (Papinot, 1948:751, for legend and historical background).

Remarks: This was a personal gift from Ido Tsushima-no-kami and Izawa Mimasaka-no-kami to Perry at Shimoda, 9 June 1854. It was entered as *kagami* 鏡 (mirror) in the KORL (*BGKM,* 1914, volume 6, page 310). Neither the HNL nor the Japanese NGL include this item. An entry for *"hassun kagami"* 八寸鏡 (lit. eight inch mirror) is in the list of articles procured for the American expedition party at Shimoda (*BGKM,* 1916, volume 8, page 552). The 1859-ACB and 1953-AL each list a "mirror with case." The case is missing. It was exhibited at the Japan Society, New York City, in 1969.

USNM ECC 273

92 Temple bell (*bonshō* 梵鐘 ; *tsurigane* 釣鐘)
USNM ECC 273
H: 47 cm, D: 26 cm, W: 12.76 kg

Description: Buddhist temple bell cast in alloys of copper and zinc, with gold dusted on the exterior surface.

Characteristics: The cylindrical body, with a conical crown or *ryōzu* (also *ryūzu*) 龍頭 (lit. dragon head), was designed as a *tsurigane* (hanging bell) for suspension in a specially constructed belfry. It is ornamented with the following traditional Buddhist symbols. The upper waist, or *chi no ma* 乳の間 (breast section), is divided into four squares, each containing twelve *chi* or *nyū* 乳 (lit. breasts) for a total of 48 raised knobs (*NKDJ,* 1976, volume 18, page 244, gives the special terms associated with Buddhist legends for various parts of temple bells). The knobs are said to represent the snails that clustered themselves on Buddha's head to shield him from sunstroke (Densmore, 1927:9). Two slightly raised circles (4.5 cm in diameter), decorated with the sacred "wheel of the law" in relief, are placed just above the bead lines on opposite sides of the bell and serve as *tsukiza* 撞座 (striking seats). A curvilinear arabesque band ornaments the bead lines above the bell mouth. The bell is suspended by a loop formed by uniting the pair of trident-shape dragon heads at the apex of the bell. It is struck with a *shumoku* 撞木 (a wooden stick covered with leather or cloth). Morse (1917, volume 1, page 80) illustrates the method of hanging such a bell and the round stick with which it is struck. The incised inscription on the head of the bell states that it was "*mei suwa ichi* [?] *koku* [?]" 名諏訪一刻 (carved by the renowned first generation of Suwa 諏訪 family?). Wakayama (1967:194) identifies Suwa as a metal carver's patronymic in the province of Higo 肥後 (modern Kumamoto prefecture). The temple bell is used for tolling the time or to exorcise evil. In earlier days, it is said, temple bells were rung 108 times each morning and evening, on New Year's Eve, or on certain special occasions in order to cast out evil. The 108 peals signified the Buddhist concept of 108 worldly concerns (DeGaris, 1947, volume 2, page 67).

Remarks: This was one of the items included in the list of additional gifts presented at Shimoda in June, 1854. It was entered as a "*shōshō*" 小鐘 (small bell) in the *BGKM* (1914, volume 6, page 311), as a "gong" in both the 1859-ACB and the 1953-AL, but correctly entered in the ECC as a "large bell." It was exhibited at the Japan Society, New York City, in 1969.

Swords and Arms

93 Short samurai sword (*wakizashi* 脇差；脇指)
USNM ECC 115
Overall L: 60 cm
Blade L: 46 cm

Description: Wakizashi (lit. side thrust) steel blade in wooden sheath.

Characteristics: The *saya* 鞘 (sheath) is made of *hō no ki* 朴の木 (magnolia wood). The *wakizashi* is a shorter, companion sword that is worn with the *katana* 刀 (long fighting sword). The cutting edge of the *wakizashi* faces upward and is secured by the wearer's girdle. With no sheath ornamentation, and without the companion *kozuka* 小柄 (small knife) or *kōgai* 笄 (skewer), the *wakizashi* is a good example of the common, undecorated *shintō* 新刀 (new sword) produced during the Tokugawa period (1603–1867). As a pair, the *katana* and *wakizashi* are known as *daishō* 大小 (lit. great and little), and the wearing of the two swords was the jealously guarded prerogative of the Edo period *samurai*. The *wakizashi* was allowed to be worn in the interior of a friend's house, but the *katana* was required to be left on a special rack in the vestibule (for types of swords and sword etiquette, see Newman and Ryerson, 1964:117–119). The wearing of swords at court ceremonies was prohibited in 1868 by Emperor Meiji (H.R. Robinson, 1969:52), and the 1877 imperial edict that abolished the *samurai* class brought an end to the wearing of two swords (Newman and Ryerson, 1964:118). The sword is signed "Echizen [no] *kami* Sukehiro" 越前守助廣 ([made by] Sukehiro, the master swordsmith of the Echizen district [modern Fukui prefecture]). Sukehiro was a prominent, mid-17th century swordsmith (Wakayama, 1967:645). He was the foster father of Tsuta Sukehiro 津田助廣, another noted Edo swordsmith, according to information supplied in 1972 by the Nihon bijutsu tōken hozon kyōkai 日本美術刀剣保存協会 (Society for the Preservation of Japanese Art Swords) of the Tōken Hakubutsukan 刀剣博物館 (Sword Museum), Tokyo. It was certified (certificate 259090) by the society as *tokubetsu kichō tōken* 特別貴重刀剣 (especially valuable sword) (cf. ECC). The signature was re-examined in 1976 and was determined to be that of Tsuta Sukehiro (cf. ECC), the son who was active ca. 1660 (Wakayama, 1967:645).

Remarks: This is possibly one of the two short swords presented to Perry by the reception commissioners, Ido

Tsushima-no-kami and Izawa Mimasaka-no-kami, as additional gifts in June 1854 at Shimoda. The entry for two *tantō* 短刀 (lit. short swords) in the Shimoda gift list (cf. Appendix III) may be a rather loose reference to the *wakizashi*. A more precise, technical usage of *tantō* would refer to daggers. It was exhibited by the Division of Armed Forces History at the then Museum of History and Technology, now the National Museum of American History, Smithsonian Institution, during 1965–1969. Subsequently, it was shown at the Pacific Heritage Museum, San Francisco, in 1987.

94 Short samurai sword (*wakizashi*)
USNM ECC 116
Overall L: 77.5 cm
Blade L: 54 cm

Description: A wakizashi in magnolia wood sheath (cf. entry 93 for the manner of wearing with a companion long sword, its use as a status symbol for the wearer, associated etiquette, etc.).

Characteristics: There is no sheath ornamentation. The sword is signed "Musashi [no] daijō Fujiwara Tadahiro Nigatsu Kitsujitsu" 武蔵大掾藤原忠廣二月吉日 ([Made by] Fujiwara Tadahiro of Hizen 肥前 [modern Saga prefecture] on an auspicious day in the month of February [post-1624]). Tadahiro added the title Musashi daijō to his name in 1624 and continued to use this signature until 1632 according to the information supplied by the Nihon bijutsu tōken hozon kyōkai (cf. entry 93). It was certified (certificate 259089) as *tokubetsu kichō tōken* in 1972 (cf. ECC). Tadahiro was a renowned early 17th century swordsmith who enjoyed the patronage of the powerful Nabeshima 鍋島 family of Saga *han* 佐賀藩 (Wakayama, 1967:216).

Remarks: This sword possibly is one of two short swords that were received from Ido and Izawa at Shimoda (cf. entry 93 for description of the other short sword).

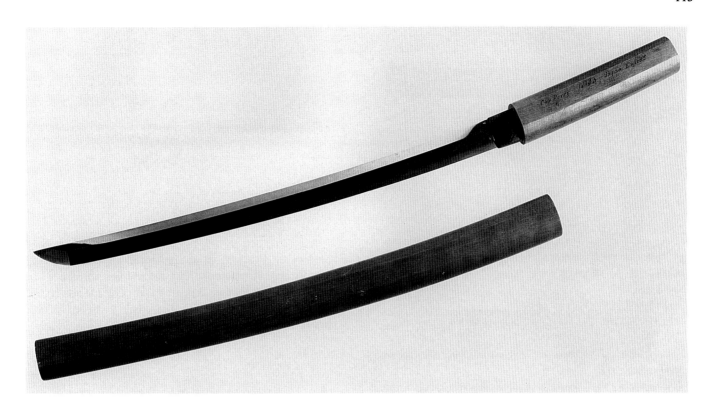

USNM ECC 115

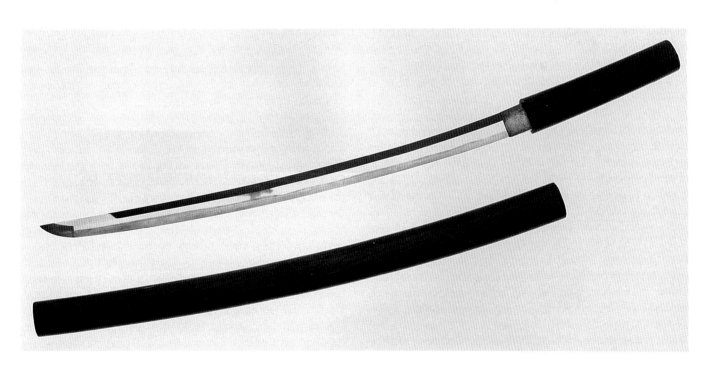

USNM ECC 116

USNM ECC 207

95 Polearm with sheathed blade (*naginata to naginata-bukuro* 長刀と長刀袋)
USNM ECC 207
Overall L: 255 cm
Blade: L: 53.5 cm

Description: Naginata (lit. long sword; sword for mowing down [enemies]).

Characteristics: The long and slightly back-curved steel blade is in the *unokubi-zukuri* 鵜頸作 (shaped like the neck of a cormorant) style (Yumoto, 1958:181; *NKDJ*, 1976, volume 2, page 713). The blade is inserted at the end of a long, slightly oval, cross-sectioned, wooden shaft. Inlaid mother-of-pearl decorates the upper 48 cm segment of the shaft, over which is mounted five cast iron bands that are finely inlaid with silver. The width of the bands varies from 1 to 7.5 cm. Heart-shape openwork in the wider bands symbolicly represents the boar's eye, "an auspicious charm, for the eye of the boar is unswerving, his charge always looking straight ahead at his foe" (H.R. Robinson, 1969:47). The hilt's *tsuka-ito* つか糸 (binding cord) is gilded. The lower end of the shaft is shod with a lunule iron fitting. The wooden *naginata-bukuro* (lit. bag for *naginata;* sheath; scabbard) is in the same shape as the blade. Its pebbled exterior is lacquered in black. Sieboldt (1973:57) described a similar specimen as "a long pike, its steel head incased in a beautifully lacquered sheath." Use of *naginata* in battle was common especially during the *sen'goku jidai* 戦国時代 (1490–1600), or "the country at war period" (B.W. Robinson, 1961:20). During the Edo period (1603–1867), *naginata* continued to be used as ceremonial weapons in formal processions and as an ornate weapon designed especially for use by women for self defense (*NKDJ*, 1976, volume 15, page 218; H.R. Robinson, 1969:47; pers. comm. Okada, conversation, March 1979). H.R. Robinson (1969, color pl. 29) illustrates an Edo period woman's *naginata* of identical design, which now is in the collection of the Museo Orientale, Venice).

Remarks: This sword has been variously identified as a "sword-like spear ornamented with scabbard" (1859-ACB, 1953-AL), a halberd (Yumoto, 1958:181), a pike (Sieboldt, 1973:57), and a glaive (B.W. Robinson, 1961:29). It was entered as an *engetsutō* 偃月刀 (lit. crescent-shape sword, a poetic variant for *naginata*) in the list of additional gifts presented to the American expedition party by Ido and Izawa at Shimoda in June 1854 (*BGKM,* 1914, volume 6, page 310; cf. Appendix III).

96 Lance with scabbard (*yari to hadome* 槍と刀止め)
USNM ECC 208
Overall L: 283 cm
Steel head: L: 26.3 cm

Description: A *yari* (type of polearm) consisting of a long, straight, wooden shaft inserted into a *kuchigane* 口金 (metal ferrule) fitting and then mounted into a heavy triangular steel head, or *moroha* 諸刃 (lit. multi-cutting edged blade) (Yumoto, 1958:91, for the term).

Characteristics: Below the ferrule is a *sendanmaki* 千段巻 (lit. ribbing for one thousand ribs) of 42.5 cm, which is lacquered in dark vermilion. The *dōrin* 胴輪 (lit. torso ring) adjoins the *sendanmaki* and serves as the hilt. The *tsuka-ito* (binding cord) is gilded (*NKDJ*, 1976, volume 19, page 591, for the technical terms for various parts of *yari*). The lower end of the shaft is fitted with a brass ferrule and a blunt iron tip through which a hole has been pierced. Ornamental, heart-shape openwork in the metal fittings represent the boar's eye, an auspicious symbol commonly used in decorating Japanese armour and weapons furniture (pers. comm. Okada, conversation, March 1979; H.R. Robinson, 1969:47, for symbolism). The *hadome* (parrying bar) is in the *shirasaya* 白鞘 (plain wood scabbard) style (Yumoto, 1958:181), and the black lacquered sheath is made of bark-like material with multiple creases. *Yari* were used both in battle and martial processions.

Remarks: This lance was received from Ido and Izawa at Shimoda in June 1854. It was included in the list of additional Japanese presents (*BGKM,* 1914, volume 6, page 310; cf. Appendix III) and was identified as a "plain spear with scabbard" in the 1859-ACB, the 1953-AL, and the ECC, which was when its blade was noted as missing.

115

USNM ECC 208 (entire lance with scabbard)

USNM ECC 208 (detailed view of lance head,
ribbing, torso ring, and scabbard)

Tools

97 Wood chisel (*nomi* 鑿)
USNM ECC 359
Overall L: 26.0 cm
Blade L: 7.9 cm, W: 4.1 cm

Description: Heavy, firm chisel with bevelled, rectangular steel blade.

Characteristics: The blade has convex shoulders and a solid, conical neck that ends in a short tapered tang, which is square in cross section. The hardwood (oak, pers. comm. Tanabe, conversation, June 1979) handle is secured to the tang with a cast iron section, or neck ferrule. The end ferrule, presumably of similar construction, is missing. An illegible maker's mark is stamped on the top blade bevel at the neck. The partly legible *sumi* inscriptions on the handle in *kanji* 漢字 (Chinese characters) and in *katakana* 片仮名 (the square form of the Japanese phonetic syllabary) read: "*Issun tsukau nomi maruu* [?]" 一寸仕ウノミマルウ [illegible] (chisel for 1 inch use, Morrow [?]). Apparently, it was inscribed by a native Japanese, possibly by an interpreter.

Remarks: The chisel was purchased by Dr. James Morrow, the scientist attached to Perry's Japan Expedition, at Hakodate in May 1854 (see Morrow in Cole, 1947:179, for his 20 May diary entry). He listed it as a "one inch & four tenths chisel" in his list of items purchased at Hakodate (cf. Appendix IV). It was exhibited at the Japan Society, New York City, in 1969.

98 Wood chisel (*nomi*)
USNM ECC 360
Overall L: 26.3 cm
Blade L: 8.0 cm, W: 2.5 cm

Description: Firm chisel with bevelled, rectangular steel blade.

Characteristics: The blade's convex shoulders and solid conical neck end in a short, tapered tang. The hardwood (oak, pers. comm. Tanabe, conversation, June 1979) handle is secured to the tang with a cast iron neck ferrule, and the end ferrule is also in cast iron. *Sumi* inscriptions on the handle read: "*hachibu tsuka no [mi] maru* [?]" 八分仕マルウ? (eight *bu* [three fourth inch] chisel, Morrow [?]). Apparently, the inscription was handwritten by a native Japanese.

Remarks: The chisel was purchased by Dr. James Morrow, the Perry expedition scientist, at Hakodate in May 1854 (see Morrow in Cole, 1947:179, for his 20 May diary entry). He entered it as a "3/4 inch chisel" in his list of items purchased in Hakodate (cf. Appendix IV).

99 Chisel (*nomi*)
USNM ECC 367
Overall L: 24.7 cm
Blade L: 12.9 cm, W: 1.2 cm

Description: Steel sash mortise with slightly collared neck.

Characteristics: The neck tang is inserted into a hardwood (oak, pers. comm. Tanabe, conversation, June 1979) handle. The neck and end ferrules are of iron. The *sumi* inscription on the handle reads: "*yombu kiri [ni] tsukau no [mi] marou* [?]" 四分切り仕ウノ［ミ］マロウ [?] (Quarter *sun* [Japanese inch, which is ~1.9 Western inches] cutting chisel Morrow [?]). Two illegible characters and the maker's trade mark are stamped on the bevelled upper surface of the blade.

Remarks: The chisel was purchased by Dr. James Morrow at Hakodate in May 1854 (see Morrow in Cole, 1947:179, for his 20 May diary entry). It was included in the list of the items purchased at Hakodate (cf. Appendix IV). Entry 103 of the ML records 11 chisels of different sizes, as does the 1953-AL. Missing are chisels ECC 364, 365, and 369.

100 Chisel (*nomi*)
USNM ECC 368
Overall L: 25.3 cm
Blade L: 12.9 cm, W: 0.6 cm

Description: Mortise chisel with steel blade and slightly collared neck.

Characteristics: The tang is inserted into a hardwood (oak, pers. comm. Tanabe, conversation, June 1979) handle. The neck and end ferrules are of iron. The Japanese inscription in *sumi* on the handle is illegible.

Remarks: This item was purchased by Dr. James Morrow at Hakodate in May 1854 (see Morrow in Cole, 1947:179, for his 20 May diary entry). It was identified as a "six tenths inch chisel" in the list of chisels purchased at Hakodate (cf. Appendix IV).

101 Wood chisel (*nomi*)
USNM ECC 362
Overall L: 25.5 cm
Blade L: 7.5 cm, W: 1.0 cm

Description: Narrow, firm chisel.

Characteristics: The bevelled, rectangular iron blade, with convex shoulders and conical neck, ends in a square,

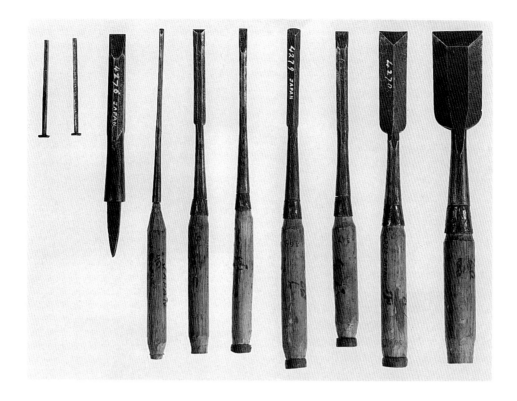

From left to right: USNM ECC 355 (2 specimens), ECC 366, ECC 363, ECC 362, ECC 368, ECC 367, ECC 360, ECC 359

cross-sectioned tang. The hardwood (oak, pers. comm. Tanabe, conversation, June 1979) handle is fitted with a roughly cast iron ferrule. The end ferrule is missing. Illegible inscriptions in *sumi* are on the handle. It is identified as a *hira-nomi* 平鑿 (lit. flat or plain chisel) (see Janata, 1965, entry 545, for a similar specimen).

Remarks: The chisel was purchased by Dr. James Morrow at Hakodate in May 1854 (see Morrow in Cole, 1947:179, for his 20 May diary entry). It was included in his list of various items purchased at Hakodate as a "triming knife chisel" (cf. Appendix IV). The chisel was exhibited at the Japan Society, New York City, in 1969.

102   Chisel (*nomi*)
USNM ECC 363
Overall L: 26.0 cm
Blade L: 8.4 cm, W: 0.4 cm

Description: Mortise chisel with narrow, rectangular steel blade.

Characteristics: The slightly indented shoulders adjoin a solid conical neck that ends in a short tapered tang, which is square in cross section. Both the neck and end ferrules are missing. The inscriptions in *sumi* on the cylindrical hardwood (oak, pers. comm. Tanabe, conversation, June 1979) handle are illegible.

Remarks: The chisel was purchased by Dr. James Morrow at Hakodate in May 1854 (see Morrow in Cole, 1947:179, for his 20 May diary entry). It was entered as a "two tenths inch chisel" in the list of items purchased at Hakodate (cf. Appendix IV).

103   Chisel blade (*nomi no ha* 鑿の刃 [先])
USNM ECC 366
Overall L: 13.2 cm, W: 1.4 cm
Tang L: 4.2 cm

Description: Mortise chisel blade of heavy steel with slightly collared neck.

Characteristics: The tapered tang is square in cross section. The maker's mark and two illegible characters are stamped on the bevelled surface of the blade.

Remarks: This item was purchased by Dr. James Morrow at Hakodate in May 1854 (see Morrow in Cole, 1947:179, for his 20 May diary entry).

104 Chisel handle (*nomi e* 鑿柄)
USNM ECC 361 (not illustrated)
L: 12 cm, D: 2 cm

Description: Cylindrical hardwood (oak, pers. comm. Tanabe, conversation, June 1979) chisel handle with an iron ferrule.

Characteristics: The inscription in *sumi* on the handle, apparently written by a Japanese, is undecipherable. The blade and neck ferrule are missing.

105 Nail (*kugi* 釘)
USNM ECC 355 (13 small-size nails; 3 large-size nails)
L: 5 cm (small size); L: 7.8 cm (large size)

Description: *Kana kakukugi* 鉄角釘 (angulated iron nail) made of a square-cut strip of iron with a tapered end.

Characteristics: The uses of *kakukugi* (lit. angulated nail) were varied and depended upon the nail's size and the materials from which it was manufactured. Wooden and bamboo nails of similar types were used for woodcrafts (Hickman and Fetchko, 1977, entry 78, for illustration). The introduction of the so-called *marukugi* 丸釘 (round nail) is considered to be a Western import (Ōtsuki, volume 2, page 5; *NKDJ*, 1976, volume 4, page 415). A flat square head is brazed to the large-size nail.

Remarks: The nails were purchased by Dr. James Morrow at Hakodate in May 1854. The ML lists them as "paper black nails" (see Morrow in Cole, 1947:179; cf. Appendix IV). They were identified in the ECC as "cut nails."

USNM ECC 364 (left), ECC 356 (top right), ECC 333 (bottom right)

106 Iron hook (*kagi* 鉤)
USNM ECC 333
L: 4 cm, H: 4 cm

Description: Right-angled iron hook made of a square-cut thin strip with a tapered end, and a thin, flat oval head brazed to the upright portion.

Characteristics: The similarity of the iron hook to what is called a "T-headed nail" (Hume, 1976:253) is striking, and the Japanese use of hook-nails probably is basically the same.

Remarks: This hook was one of two hooks included in the list of Japanese carpenters' tools purchased by Dr. James Morrow in May 1854 at Hakodate (Morrow in Cole, 1947:176, 231, for his 10 May [1854] diary entry and for the list of items; cf. Appendix IV). Only one iron hook now remains. It was identified as an "iron hat hook?" in the 1859-ACB, the 1953-AL, and in the ECC.

107 Gimlet (*kiri* 錐)
USNM ECC 364
Overall L: 23.4 cm
Handle L: 20.2 cm, D: 1.3 cm

Description: Short, thin, and triangular iron point.
Characteristics: The point is inserted into a cylindrical wooden (oak, pers. comm. Tanabe, conversation, June 1979) handle.

Remarks: This is one of a number of varied-size chisels and other items purchased in Hakodate by Dr. James Morrow (Morrow in Cole, 1947:176, for his diary entry for 10 May [1854]; ML entry, "small chisel," in Appendix IV). It was identified in the 1859-ACB and in the 1953-AL as a very small-size chisel, but in the ECC it is listed as an awl.

108 Brass hinges (*dō chōtsugai* 銅蝶番)
USNM ECC 356
L: 4.8 cm, W: 1.5 cm

Description: Two rectangular brass plates hinged together along their length with an iron hinge pin.

Characteristics: Each hinge plate bears five nail holes and an indentation of a quarter circle in the two corners away from the hinge. The term *chōtsugai* (lit. butterfly joints) is said to originate from the shape of the hinges, which resemble that of a butterfly (*NKDJ,* 1976, volume 13, page 527).

Remarks: This item probably was purchased or given informally. Only the AWL has an entry for iron and other metal products (*BGKM,* 1914, volume 6, page 198).

109 Cutting iron for carpenter's plane (*kanna no ha* 鉋の刃)
USNM ECC 372
L: 11 cm, W: 1.8 cm, T: 0.8 cm

Description: ECC 372 is a knife-shape cutting iron made of steel with a dull edge.

Characteristics: This cutting iron is specifically designed for *hidari-wakitori kanna* 左脇取り鉋 (lit. leftside scraping plane), which is used for smoothing or shaping the left side of a given object (Janata, 1965, entry 538, for the term and illustration). This type of cutting iron stands vertically in the wooden stock (Morse, 1886:38–39, for various types of Japanese carpenter's tools and illustrations).

Remarks: This is one of two plane bits purchased in Hakodate, 1854, by Dr. James Morrow (Morrow in Cole, 1947:176, 231, for his 10 May [1854] journal entry and for the list of materials purchased in Hakodate, which includes an entry for a "small bit for plane"; cf. Appendix IV). It was identified as a "carpenter's hone" in the 1859-ACB, the 1953-AL, and in the ECC.

USNM ECC 372 (illustrating both sides of cutting iron)

USNM ECC 358 (illustrating both sides of cutting iron)

110   Cutting iron for carpenter's plane (*kanna no ha*)
USNM ECC 358
L: 11.8 cm, W: 6.8 cm, T: 0.7 cm

Description: ECC 358 is a slightly larger but otherwise identical cutting iron to that of entry 109 (ECC 357).

Characteristics: A partially legible, incised inscription reads: "*Dai* Watanabe *honten* Hirabe [?]" [the main shop of the great Watanabe Hirabe] 大 渡辺本店 平兵衛 [?], plus △, which is a trade mark (see Kurihara, 1901:187–189, for common types of trade marks).

Remarks: This tool was purchased in Hakodate, 1854, by Dr. James Morrow (Morrow in Cole, 1947:176, 231, for his journal entry for 10 May [1854] and for the list of items purchased in Hakodate, which includes an entry for a "large bit for plane"; cf. Appendix IV).

111   Carpenter's plane (*kanna* 鉋)
USNM ECC 357
Overall L: 28.8 cm, W: 7.5 cm, H: 3.0 cm
Cutting iron L: 11.3 cm, W: 5 cm, T: 0.5 cm

Description: A type of "smoothing plane" (Jackson and Day, 1978:135, for the term) known as *daiganna* or *daikanna* 台鉋 (lit. the plane in rectangular wood block) (oak, pers. comm. Tanabe, conversation, June 1979).

Characteristics: A carpenter's plane is used for the final smoothing or shaping of plain wooden surfaces. The rectangular cutting iron is made of steel and has a round top and bevelled edge. It is inserted in an inclined slot in the wooden stock. "The Japanese carpenter draws the plane towards him instead of pushing it from him. ... Their bodies [planes], instead of being thick blocks of wood, are quite wide and thin, and the blades are inclined at a greater angle than the blade in our plane" (Morse, 1886:38). Faint illegible inscriptions in *sumi* occur on both the cutting iron and the wooden stock.

Remarks: This tool was purchased by Dr. James Morrow in Hakodate in 1854. Morrow's diary entry of 10 May [1854] states that he "also bought ... a few carpenter's tools" (Morrow in Cole, 1947:176). His "List of Specimens in Arts Manufactures, Etc. Bought in Hakodadi [Hakodate]..." records "two planes" (Morrow in Cole, 1947:231; cf. Appendix IV). This

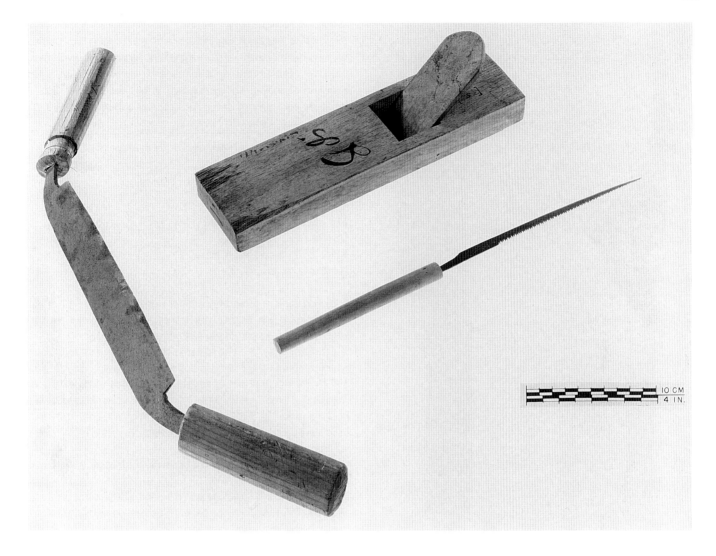

USNM ECC 347 (left), ECC 357 (top right), ECC 350 (bottom right)

plane was exhibited at the Naval Historical Foundation's Truxtun Decatur Naval Museum, Washington, D.C., in 1975–1976.

112   Draw knife (sen 鐇; sen-kanna)
USNM ECC 347
L: 50.3 cm, W: 4 cm

Description: Single-edge straight iron blade formed with a tang at each end that inserts at an oblique angle into a cylindrical wooden handle.

Characteristics: The flat blade is bevelled on the top front edge only. The main use of a draw knife is to shape lumber sections roughly to size before applying a plane (Jackson and Day, 1978:174).

Remarks: This knife was purchased at Hakodate by Dr. James Morrow, 10 May 1854 (Morrow in Cole, 1947:176, for

his 10 May [1854] journal entry; also cf. Appendix IV). It was exhibited at the Japan Society, New York City, in 1969. It also was included in the "Men Who Made the Navy" exhibit at the Truxtun Decatur Naval Museum, Washington, D.C., in 1975–1976.

113   Saw (nokogiri 鋸)
USNM ECC 350
Overall L: 36.0 cm, W: 1.0 cm
Blade L: 21.0 cm

Description: A *mawashinoko* 廻しのこ (compass saw) with a narrow steel blade inserted into a straight, cylindrical wood handle (oak, pers. comm. Tanabe, conversation, June 1979).

Characteristics: Also known as a keyhole saw, the compass saw with its chisel-like teeth is designed to cut curves

USNM ECC 320

USNM ECC 351

(Japanese cedar, pers. comm. Tanabe, conversation, June 1979). The length of the handle is approximately the same as the saw itself (Janata, 1965, entry 526; Morse, 1917, volume 2, page 39, for similar specimens and method of use). This compass saw was not entered in either the official lists of Japanese presents nor in the AWL. It was exhibited at the Japan Society, New York City, in 1969.

114 Kitchen knife (*hōchō* 包丁)
USNM ECC 320
Blade L: 17.5 cm, W: 4.7 cm
Handle L: 12 cm, D: 3 cm

Description: Common *nakiri-bōchō* 菜切り包丁 (lit. kitchen knife for cutting vegetables) consisting of a parallel-edged, thin but broad blade with a rounded end.

Characteristics: The blade is inserted into a straight, oval, wooden handle (pine, pers. comm. Tanabe, conversation, June 1979) (for illustrations of several other types of *nakiri-bōchō*, see Janata, 1965, entries 343, 345). *Hōchō* is an abbreviation of *hōchō-gatana* 包丁刀 (lit. knife for cookery), but it often is used as a generic term for all kitchen knives (*NKDJ*, 1976, volume 18, page 64).

Remarks: This item probably was purchased at the bazaar held in Shimoda. The AWL includes an entry for "*tetsu narabi ni hagane mono*" 鉄並鋼物 (iron and other metal products) (*BGKM*, 1914, volume 6, page 198), but none of the official lists of Japanese presents includes a kitchen knife. It was exhibited at the Japan Society, New York City, in 1969.

115 Hoe blade (*kuwa-saki* 鍬先)
USNM ECC 376
L: 24.8 cm, W: 12.3 cm

Description: Straight-edge, rectangular *kuwa-saki* (lit. front end of a hoe), or iron hoe blade, tapering at the back end into a looped shank.

Characteristics: A long, cylindrical, wooden handle is inserted, when in use, at right angles into the looped shank.

Remarks: This probably was a purchased item. The SML has an entry for "*kuwa*" (hoe) (*BGKM*, 1916, volume 8, page 555), and the AWL includes "*nōgu no hinagata*" 農具の雛型 (samples of agricultural implements) (*BGKM*, 1914, volume 6, page 202).

or holes in a panel. Similar saws have been identified as *hikimawashinoko* ひきまわしのこ (Hickman and Fetchko, 1977:77) and *mawashibiki* まわしびき (Janata, 1965:113, entry 531).

Remarks: The list of articles purchased by Dr. James Morrow at Hakodate in 1854 includes "one small ripping saw" (cf. Appendix IV); however, this item may refer to ECC 351, a common type of a small handsaw (*tatehikinoko* 縦引きのこ) (L: 42 cm, W: 3.7 cm) with a parallel-edge square iron blade that is inserted into a straight, cylindrical, wooden handle

USNM ECC 376

USNM ECC 381

116 Ploughshare (*suki no saki* 鋤の先)
USNM ECC 381
L: 24 cm, W: 16.2 cm

Description: *Suki no saki* (lit. the front edge of plough; metal ploughshare), or, in the Aomori dialect of northern Japan, *suki-nomi* (*NKDJ,* 1976, volume 11, page 371), made of cast iron.

Characteristics: The blade is broad in shape but has a tapered point and a square-cut molded hollow that is edged to fit over the wooden body of the plough. It possibly is a Ryūkyūan variety (Janata, 1965, entry 191, for a similar type).

Remarks: This probably was a purchased item. The SML includes the word "*suki*" (*BGKM,* 1916, volume 8, page 555), and the AWL has an entry for "*nōgu no hinagata.*" It was entered in both the 1859-ACB and the 1953-AL as a "cast-iron ploughshare point." This piece was exhibited at the Japan Society, New York City, in 1969.

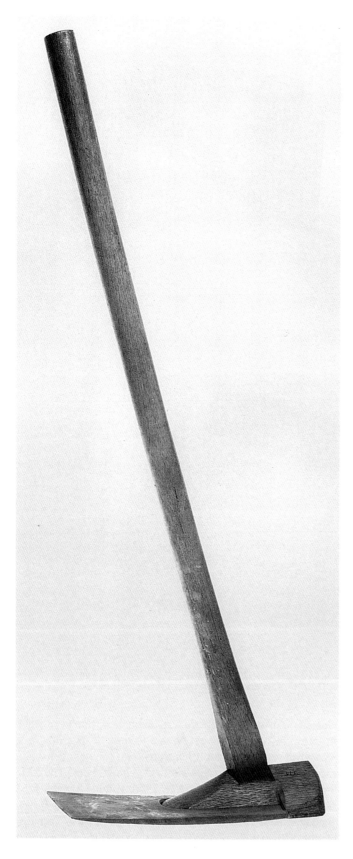

USNM ECC 375

117 Ploughshare (*suki no saki*)
USNM ECC 379 (not illustrated)
L: 26 cm, W: 14.1 cm

Description: Cast-iron, slightly convex-edged rectangular blade with U-shape cut in the back.
Characteristics: The back is split at the edges for insertion of a wooden handle (not present).
Remarks: This piece probably was purchased by Dr. James Morrow, either at Hakodate or at Shimoda, or it may have been received as an informal gift. The AWL has an entry for "*nōgu no hinagata*" (cf. Appendix V). It was entered in both the 1859-ACB and the 1953-AL as a spade, and it was identified in the ECC as "spade blade."

118 Hoe (*kuwa* 鍬)
USNM ECC 375
L: 90.0 cm

Description: *Kuwagara* 鍬柄 , hoe with a long handle (*NKDJ*, 1976, volume 7, page 43, for the standard term and other local variants).
Characteristics: The hoe is constructed of a heavy and slightly oval wooden stick (oak, pers. comm. Tanabe, conversation, June 1979) that fits into a triangular cross section of wood block. The front end of the rectangular block is rounded and bevelled. The *kuwasaki* (metal blade) slides onto the bevelled part of the block.
Remarks: The hoe was purchased by the Rev. George Jones, chaplain of the *Mississippi*, at a bazaar held on 21 June 1854 in Shimoda. Dr. James Morrow reimbursed the Rev. Jones the cost from "the money fund of the Department of Interior" (Morrow in Cole, 1947:203, for his 23 June diary entry). The ML includes an entry for "June, Japanese hoe" (cf. Appendix IV). Morrow listed it as a desired sample specimen (Morrow in Cole, 1947:250), and the AWL included an entry for "*nōgu no hinagata*" (cf. Appendix V; *BGKM*, 1914, volume 6, page 202). It was identified as a large-size hoe in both the 1859-ACB and 1953-AL.

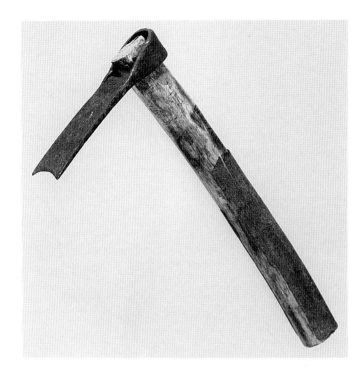

USNM ECC 384

119 Hoe (*kuwa*)
USNM ECC 384
L: 27.0 cm

Description: *Tekuwa* 手鍬 (hand hoe) with an iron blade and a short, straight, wooden handle.

Characteristics: The blade has a slightly concave edge and a loop at the back through which is inserted the wooden handle. A *tekuwa* commonly is used for weeding.

Results: The hoe was purchased by the Rev. George Jones, chaplain of the *Mississippi,* 21 June 1854, at a bazaar held in Shimoda. The purchase was made on behalf of Dr. James Morrow (Morrow in Cole, 1947:203, 233, for his 23 June journal entry, and for an entry for a Japanese hoe that was included in the specimens purchased in Shimoda). It was listed as one of the agricultural sample specimens desired (Morrow in Cole, 1947:250), as reflected in the AWL entry "*nōgu no hinagata*" (*BGKM,* 1914, volume 6, page 202). It was identified as a "hand hoe for beans" in both the 1859-ACB and the 1953-AL but was recorded as a "small digger" in the ECC.

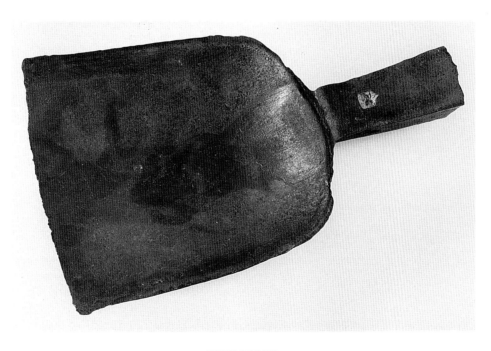

USNM ECC 288

120 Shovel (*shaberu* シャベル)
USNM ECC 288
L: 23.5 cm, W: 15.5 cm

Description: Square mouth, cast-iron shovel blade with hollow-handle shank.

Characteristics: The Japanese term, *shaberu,* indicates that the tool's design and concept was of European origin.

Remarks: This item probably was purchased by Dr. James Morrow at Shimoda in June 1854. The entry, "spade," in the list of items purchased at Shimoda may refer to this shovel (cf. Appendix IV).

USNM ECC 388

From left to right: USNM ECC 386, ECC 387, ECC 385

121 Sickle (*kama* 鎌)
USNM ECC 385–388
various sizes

Description: *Te-gama* 手鎌 (hand sickle) in a variety of sizes and shapes.

Characteristics: Only the hand-sickle blade (L: 26 cm, W: 7.2 cm) remains of ECC 385. The blade is composed of a wide, curved, single-edge iron blade with the sharp edge on the inside of the curve. The blade ends in an open shank. ECC 386 (L: 51 cm, W: 5 cm) has a slightly curved iron blade that tapers to a point. The sharp edge of the blade is on the inside of the curve. The flat back end is inserted, through an iron ferrule, into a split in the straight wooden handle. ECC 387 is a type of hand sickle known as a bill hook (L: 49 cm, W: 7 cm). The short, broad blade is inserted, through an iron ferrule, into the short, straight wooden handle. ECC 388 is a hand sickle or hand scythe (L: 45.8 cm, W: 2.8 cm) that consists of a long narrow iron blade with a pronounced curve toward the tip and a serrated cutting edge. The blade is inserted, through an iron ferrule, into a short, wooden, barrel-shape handle with carved panels to form a grip. This type of *te-gama* is used for harvesting rice; thus, it is called *inakari-kama* 稲刈鎌 (lit. rice-cutting sickle) (Janata, 1965, entry 201, for a similar tool with a longer handle).

Remarks: The sickle was listed in the SML as "*kama*" (*BGKM,* 1916, volume 8, page 555), and the AWL includes an entry for "*nōgu no hinagata*" (*BGKM,* 1914, volume 6, page 202). It was exhibited at the Japan Society, New York City, in 1969.

Miscellany

122 Doll (*nin'gyō* 人形)
USNM ECC 161
H: 9.5 cm, W: 8 cm

Description: Seated *gosho nin'gyō* 御所人形 (palace doll) figure of a boy.

Characteristics: This doll is made of clay that is coated with a thick application of *gofun* 胡粉 (levigated oyster shell) mixed with *nikawa* 膠 (isinglass, a glue-like substance) to provide a highly glossy white surface. The eyes, nose, mouth, and body front are painted. Two round pieces of black cloth are pasted on both sides of the top of the head, along with painted hair strands. The doll wears the traditional *haragake* 腹掛け (a bib-like piece of cloth that covers the front of the body of a child and ties behind the neck and waist) in a painted floral design. Held in its left arm is a decorated gourd, which includes an image of a turtle. An inscription in gold on back of the turtle reads: "*kin ōshō*" 金王将 (lit. gold general). The term "gold general" refers to a high ranking chessman in the game of *shōgi* 将棋 . The *ō* 王 (king) and gold generals retain their rank throughout the game and are guarded by other pieces (Culin, 1958:90–91). Edo period palace dolls were produced in Kyoto and traditionally were given as gifts by members of the Imperial household and other nobles. They often were used as charms against misfortune and sometimes were placed in household shrine altars to solicit the favor of the gods for a good harvest (Boger, 1964:305–306, for use of palace dolls). The inscription may allude to the venerable rank of the recipient, especially with respect to the symbolism ascribed to the title.

Remarks: The doll probably was received from Izawa Mimasaka-no-kami. The HNL and PJL each includes an entry for "8 boxes, 13 dolls" (cf. Appendixes I, II). It was entered as "Japanese household gods" in the 1859-ACB and 1953-AL. The doll was described as a "plump squatting figure of a man" in the ECC.

Additional Specimens: ECC 159 and 160 have slightly different sizes than ECC 161; however, further descriptions of them are not possible due to the extent of their deterioration.

USNM ECC 161 (front view)

USNM ECC 161 (side view)

123 Doll (*ningyō*)
USNM ECC 304, ECC 316
H: 25.3 cm, W: 7 cm

Description: Two *mitsuore-ningyō* 三折人形 (lit. three-bend doll or three-jointed doll) are figurines of smiling boys, each with a movable head (Boger, 1964:304, for origin of the term *mitsuore*).

Characteristics: With the exception of the upper arms, both dolls are made of clay that is coated with a thick application of *gofun* mixed with *nikawa* to provide a highly glossy white surface. The upper parts of the arms are constructed from ivory crepe de Chine that is covered with steel wires overlaid with cotton padding. The three flexible joints, devised of metal clasps, are at the shoulders, thighs, and knees so as to maneuver the dolls into poses of standing, bowing, and squatting in a typical Japanese manner, and also to perform acrobatic feats (Newman and Ryerson, 1964:39). Black, man-made, hair-like material is pasted on each doll's head in the fashion of an Edo period hair style known as *karako-mage* 唐子髷 (*NKDJ*, 1976, volume 5, page 189, for term). This hair style was worn by male children from infants to six years old (Boger, 1964:304). The dolls have glass eyes, red-painted lips, and open mouths showing the teeth. This type of doll, unlike other types that were used as charms or for ornamentation, was specifically designed as a child's plaything and also as a costume doll (Boger, 1964:304) that could be dressed in a variety of garb.

Remarks: The dolls were a gift from Izawa Mimasaka-no-kami. The HNL has an entry for "8 boxes, 13 dolls" (*BGKM*, 1914, volume 5, page 309). Although the KORL described the dolls as *hassun-ningyō* 八寸人形 (eight inch dolls) (*BGKM*, 1916, volume 8, pages 541–542), the NGL entry listed them as *hadaka-ningyō* 裸人形 (naked dolls) (*BGKM*, 1912, volume 4, page 560). Both the 1859-ACB and the 1953-AL listed them as "baby dolls."

Additional Specimens: ECC 305 and ECC 306 are identical to ECC 304.

124 Toy figurines (*ningyō*)
USNM ECC unnumbered (not illustrated)
H: 7.5 cm (average)

Description: A set of 65 painted miniature clay dolls, or *fushimi-ningyō* 伏見人形 (lit. dolls from the Fushimi district of Kyoto) (Boger, 1964:302, for origin of the term and popular representative types), ranging in size from 5.4 to 18.5 cm.

Characteristics: The differing sizes are due to the figurines' postures, dress, and the length of various objects that they carry. Most of the dolls represent *samurai*, footmen, and other grades of warriors. The figure of a *daimyō* 大名 (feudal lord) in a *kago* 加籠 (palanquin) also is included. From the number of pieces, the varied types of costume used to represent rank, and such equipment and regalia as umbrellas, spears, streamers, chests, food baskets, etc., this set of figurines was intended to be arranged to depict the annual processional journey of the local *daimyō* and his retinue to Edo (Sieboldt, 1973:68–71, for detailed descriptions of the travelling party and various types of equipment). Such displays of martial dolls are a common form of celebration of *tan'go* 端午, a boy's festival, which occurs on the fifth day of the fifth month (Newman and Ryerson, 1964:39, for a discussion of special types of boy's day display dolls and manners of display; Griffis, 1876:462, and H.R. Robinson, 1969:49, for the appeal of such toys to young Japanese masculinity). A very thin, painted wooden stick with a pointed end is attached to each figure, and numerals are inscribed on the sole of each bare foot, along with either *migi* 右 (right) or *hidari* 左 (left), designating the order and position in the procession.

Remarks: These dolls probably were purchased as a complete set at the Shimoda bazaar, for the AWL has an entry for "*shōni gambutsu*" 小児玩物 (children's toys) (*BGKM*, 1914, volume 6, page 201). Of the 65 dolls, 43 are broken. The number comprising a complete set is unknown.

USNM ECC 304

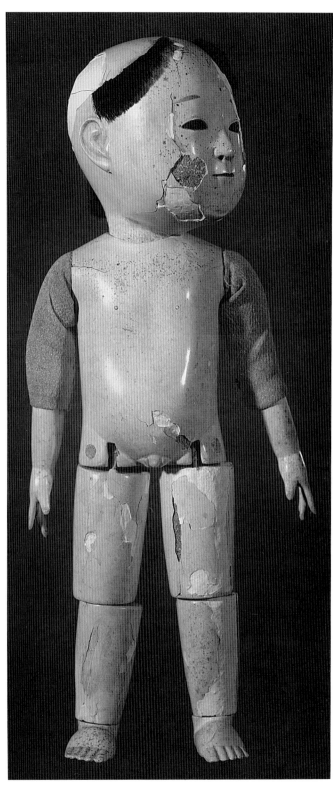

USNM ECC 316

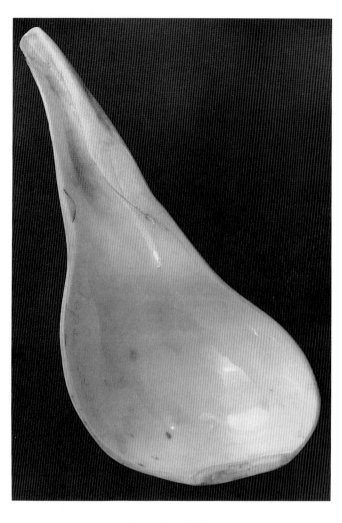

USNM ECC 167

125 Spoon (*saji* 匙)
USNM ECC 167
L: 12 cm, W: 5.5 cm

Description: A spoon made from *hora-gai* 法螺貝 (conch or trumpet shell) by cutting lengthwise through a conch shell.

Characteristics: The spoon has retained the natural pinkish beige lustre and texture of the shell. The shape of the spoon is similar to that of a Chinese soup spoon, which suggests that the article was specially designed for export or for use on special, ceremonial occasions.

Remarks: An entry in the HNL for "7 boxes cups and spoons and goblet cut from conch shells" indicates that this spoon and other similar objects were the gifts of Chief Commissioner, Hayashi Daigaku-no-kashira (Hawks, 1865). The HL also has an entry for "*saji*" (Hora, 1970:242). This spoon was exhibited at the Naval Historical Foundation's Truxtun Decatur Naval Museum, Washington, D.C., in 1975–1976.

Additional Specimens: ECC 168 is similar to ECC 167, but it has a repaired crack line between the handle and the small shallow bowl.

USNM ECC 313

126 Inkstone (*suzuri-ishi* 硯石) in wooden case
USNM ECC 313
L: 10.2 cm, W: 6.5 cm, H: 1.3 cm

Description: A slightly irregular, oval slab of stone with a greyish brown texture.

Characteristics: The ink is produced by rubbing a *sumi* (ink-stick) against the stone's surface. Close to the edge of the stone are carved two well-like, oval-shape holes called *suzuri no umi* 硯の海 (lit. the inkstone sea) or *suzuri no kenchi* 硯の硯池 (lit. the inkstone lake), which are used for holding water to mix with the ink powder. Carvings of decorative vine leaves in low relief surround the holes, giving the effect of a *uri* 乒 (melon) design sculpture. Encasing the inkstone is a dark reddish brown mahogany container with cover that is constructed to fit the stone's size.

Remarks: The inkstone was purchased by Dr. James Morrow, the expedition scientist, at Hakodate in May 1854, and it was listed in the ML as "one ink stone" (cf. Appendix IV). It was entered as an "ink stand" in the 1859-ACB and was so marked on the surface of the inkstone. The inkstone was exhibited at the Japan Society, New York City, in 1969.

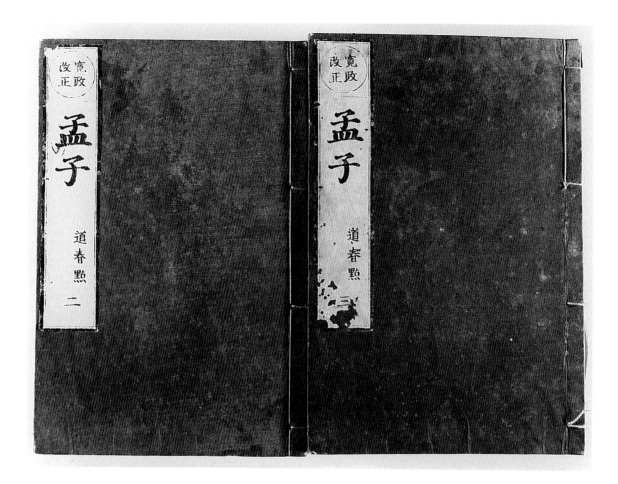

NMAH-DAF Dudley 59873-N-00103 (book cover)

127 Book (*shomotsu* 書物 ; *hon* 本)
NMAH-DAF Dudley 59873-N-00103 and 59873-N-00104
H: 26 cm, W: 17.8 cm, T: 1 cm (each volume)

Description: Volumes 2 and 3 of a woodblock print of a Chinese classic by Mencius.

Characteristics: The book is unpaginated, double leaf, and thread bound. The title on the cover reads: "*Mōshi Dōshun-ten Kansei kaisei*" 孟子道春点寛政改正 (Revised edition of Mōshi; punctuation by Dōshun, published in the Kansei period [1789–1800]). Mōshi is the Japanese reading of Meng Tzu or Mencius (371–289 BC), a Chinese philosopher of the Confucian school. Hayashi Dōshun 林道春 (1583–1657) was a famous Confucian scholar in Japan who was appointed 1st Secretary upon the founding of the Tokugawa shogunate in 1606 (see Papinot, 1948:148, for a biographical sketch). The title page imprint qualifies the edition as being "*Shu Ki shūchū*" 朱喜集註 (a variorum edition annotated by Chu Hsi (1130–1200) [a Neo-Confucian]).

Remarks: This incomplete set was purchased from a bookseller, Yoshizakiya 吉崎屋 , in Hakodate, May 1854. A notation by the collector described it as "a Japanese novel [entitled] The Orphans of Mount Tsuruga or The Cruel Uncle." The volumes were a gift of E.M. Guilmette, a descendant of the collector; they were received in 1977.

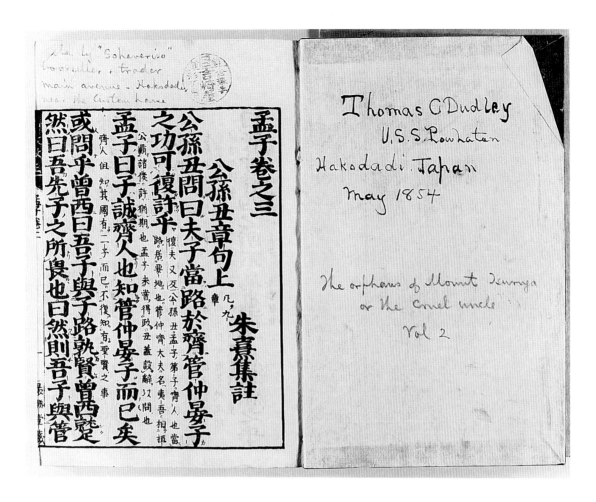

NMAH-DAF Dudley 59873-N-00103 (title page)

128 Signature (shomei 署名)
NMAH-DAF Dudley 59873-N-00120 (not illustrated)
H: 9 cm, W: 5.0 cm

Description: An autograph of Iida Keinosuke 飯田敬之助 in the traditional manner of brush writing in *sumi* on a piece of mulberry bark paper.

Characteristics: The signed bark paper was pasted on a typical-size (5×9 cm) Western style calling card. The penciled inscription in the hand of the collector reads: "Eda [Iida]

Keinosuke Colonel of a Regiment at Uraga. Visited U.S.S. Powhatan, at Yokohama March 1854."

Remarks: The NMAH-DAF Dudley collection accession list, number 1977.0186, and card catalog recorded the item as being a "calling card of Japanese colonel," which is most unlikely as use of calling cards by the Japanese began ca. 1860's and then only by a small select group of people. The signature, received in 1977, was a gift of E.M. Guilmette, a descendant of the collector.

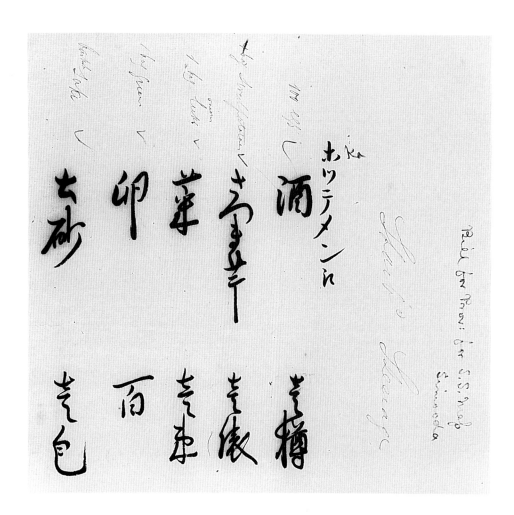

NMAH-DAF Dudley 59873-N-00160

129 Provisions list (*kyōkyū himmoku* 供給品目)
NMAH-DAF Dudley 59873-N-00160
H: 31 cm, W: 40.5 cm

Description: List of provisions supplied by the Japanese to the *Powhatan* at Shimoda in 1854.

Characteristics: The list was prepared in the traditional manner with the brush writing in *sumi* on a piece of white mulberry bark paper. The inscription reads: "Hottemen *e*" ホッテメン江 (To Portman [Anton L.C. Portman, the Dutch-Japanese interpreter, hired in Shanghai, who served as Perry's flag clerk]) (Morison, 1967:297). The provision list recorded *sake isson* 酒壱樽 (one barrel of rice wine),

satsumaimo ippyō さつま芋壱俵 (one sack of potatoes), *na issoku* 菜壱束 (one bunch of vegetables), *tamago hyaku* 卵百 (100 eggs), and *hakusha ippō* 白砂一包 (one bag of white sand). An English translation of each entry was provided, probably by the collector. The vegetables were identified as "greens," whereas the bag of sand was incorrectly translated as "one bag of onions," and the eggs as "wine." In the handwriting of the collector is written "Bill in Japanese for provisions purchased in Simoda, Japan for Starboard Steerage, *Powhatan*." No prices were given with the itemized list.

Remarks: The provision list, received in 1977, was a gift of E.M. Guilmette, a descendant of the collector.

130 Gift label (*okurimono hyōsatsu* 贈物表札)
NMAH-DAF Dudley 59873-N-0089
H: 31 cm, W: 10.8 cm

Description: Rectangular piece of thick, off-white *minogami* inscribed in Japanese, apparently used as a gift label.

Characteristics: The inscription reads: "*Tei* Potomen 呈 ポートメン [Anton L.C. Portman] Hirayama Kenjirō 平山謙次郎 [and] Aibara Isaburō" 合原緒三郎 (Presented to Portman by Hirayama Kenjirō and Aibara Isaburō). Anton L.C. Portman was the Dutch interpreter hired at Shanghai, who served as Commodore Perry's flag clerk (Morison, 1967:297). In April 1854 (cf. the collector's acquisition date below), Hirayama was a public censor assigned to the Kanagawa district. Hora (1970:169) identifies him as *Kanagawa zaikin kachi metsuke* 神奈川在勤徒目付 . Aibara, an assistant to the Uraga magistrates, is identified by Hora (1970:237) as *Uraga bugyō shihai kumi yoriki* 浦賀奉行支配組与力 . Inscribed in pencil in the hand of the collector is the incorrect translation: "List of presents from the Emperor of Japan to Mr. Portman, Tokohama [Yokohama], Jeddo [Edo] Bay, April, 1854."

Remarks: The label was received in 1977 as a gift of E.M. Guilmette, a descendant of the collector.

APPENDIXES

I. List of the Articles Received from the Japanese Government on 24 March 1854

The source for this list is Francis Hawks, 1856, *Narrative of the Expedition of an American Squadron to the China Seas and Japan, Performed in the Years 1852, 1853, and 1854, under the Command of Commodore M.C. Perry, United States Navy, by Order of the Government of the United States*, page 369.

1st. For the government of the United States of America, from the Emperor—

1 gold lacquered writing apparatus.
1 gold lacquered paper box.
1 gold lacquered book-case.
1 lacquered writing table.
1 censer of bronze (cow-shape), supporting silver flower and stand.
1 set waiters.
1 flower holder and stand.
2 brasiers.
10 pieces fine red pongee.
10 pieces white pongee.
5 pieces flowered crape.
5 pieces red dyed figured crape.

2d. From Hayashi, 1st commissioner—

1 lacquered writing apparatus.
1 lacquered paper box.
1 box of paper.
1 box flowered note paper.
5 boxes stamped note and letter paper.
4 boxes assorted sea-shells, 100 in each.
1 box of branch coral and feather in silver.
1 lacquered chow-chow box.
1 box, set of three, lacquered goblets.
7 boxes cups and spoons and goblet cut from conch shells.

3d. From Ido, 2d commissioner—

2 boxes lacquered waiters, 4 in all.
2 boxes, containing 20 umbrellas.
1 box 30 coir brooms.

4th. From Izawa, 3d commissioner—

1 piece red pongee.
1 piece white pongee.
8 boxes, 13 dolls.
1 box bamboo woven articles.
2 boxes bamboo stands.

5th. From Udono, 4th commissioner—

3 pieces striped crape.
2 boxes porcelain cups.
1 box, 10 jars of soy.

6th. From Matsuzaki, 5th commissioner—

3 boxes porcelain goblets.
1 box figured matting.
35 bundles oak charcoal.

7th. From Abe, 1st Imperial councillor [sic.]—

14 pieces striped-figured silk (taffeta).

8th.–12th. From each of [the] other 5 Imperial councillors [sic.]—

10 pieces striped-figured silk (taffeta).

13th. From [the] Emperor to Commodore Perry—

1 lacquered writing apparatus.
1 lacquered paper box.
3 pieces red pongee.
2 pieces white pongee.
2 pieces flowered crape.
3 pieces figured dyed crape.

14th. From [the] commissioners to Capt. H.A. Adams—

3 pieces plain red pongee.
2 pieces dyed figured crape.
20 sets lacquered cups and covers.

15th.–17th. From [the] commissioners to Mr. Perry, Mr. Portman, and Mr. S.W. Williams, each—

2 pieces red pongee.
2 pieces dyed figured crape.
10 sets lacquered cups and covers.

18th–22d. From [the] commissioners to Mr. Gay, Mr. Danby, Mr. Draper, Dr. Morrow, and Mr. J.P. Williams—

1 piece red dyed figured crape.
10 sets lacquered cups and covers.

23d. From [the] Emperor to the squadron—

200 bundles of rice, each 5 Japanese pecks.
300 chickens.

II. List of Presents Received from the Emperor of Japan and His High Ministers for the Government of the United States and Others

The source for this list is Roger Pineau, editor, 1968, *The Japan Expedition 1852–1854: The Personal Journal of Commodore Matthew C. Perry,* pages 194–196.

For the Government of the United States

1st. From the Emperor.

1 lacquered writing table.
1 gold " book-case.
1 " " paper box.
1 " " writing apparatus.
1 bronze censer on stand, shaped like an ox with silver flower on his back.
1 set of two lacquered trays.
1 bamboo bouquet holder and stand.
2 braziers or censers with silver tops.
10 pieces fine red pongee.
10 " fine white pongee.
5 " each figured and dyed flower crape.
2 swords and 3 matchlocks.

2nd. From Abe, Prince of Ise.

15 pieces striped and figured pongee or taffeta.

3rd to 7th. From Matsudaira and each of the other four imperial councillors.

10 pieces striped and figured pongee or taffeta silk, 50 pieces in all.

8th. From Hayashi, 1st commissioner.

1 lacquered writing apparatus.
1 lacquered paper box.
1 box flowered paper.
5 " stamped note paper.
1 " flowered note paper.
1 " branch of coral and silver feather of "byssus."
1 lacquered chow-chow box.
8 boxes cups and spoons of conch shell and shell cup.
100 kinds of seashells in 4 boxes.
1 box of 3 lacquered cups.

9th. From Ido, 2d commissioner.

2 boxes lacquered waiters, 2 in each.
2 " 20 umbrellas each.
1 " 30 coir brooms.

10th. From Izawa, 3d commissioner.

2 pieces red and white pongee.

8 boxes of 13 dolls.
1 " of bamboo ware.
2 " of bamboo low tables.

11th. From Udono, 4th commissioner.

3 pieces striped crape.
2 boxes 20 porcelain cups.
1 " soy, 10 jars.

12th. From Michitaro Matsuzaki.

3 boxes porcelain cups.
1 " figured matting.
35 bundles oak charcoal.

13th. For Commodore Perry from the Emperor.

1 lacquered writing apparatus.
1 " paper box.
3 pieces red and 2 pieces white pongee.
3 " dyed and 2 pieces flowered crape.

14th. From the commissioners for Capt. Adams.

3 pieces plain red pongee.
2 " red dyed figured crape.
20 lacquered cups and covers.

15th to 17th.—For Messrs. S.W. Williams, O.H. Perry, and A.C. Portman (to each).

2 pieces red pongee.
2 " red dyed figured crape.
10 lacquered cups and covers.

18th to 22d. For Messrs. J. Gay, R. Danby, J. Williams, J. Morrow, W.B. Draper (to each).

1 piece dyed figured crape.
10 lacquered cups and covers.

23d. For the squadron from the Emperor.

300 fowls.
200 bales rice, each 135 pounds.

24th. For United States of America from the prefect and interpreters.

5 pieces figured crape.

III. List of Japanese Reception Commissioners' Gifts Presented to the American Expedition Party on 9 June 1854 [at Shimoda]*

The source for this list is "Kokui ōsetsuroku" [The Reception Commissioners' Records Relating to the Black (ship) Barbarians (Americans)] in *Bakumatsu gaikoku kankei monjo* [BGKM], 1914, volume 6, pages 310–313.

Return Gifts for the Howitzer

From Ido Tsushima-no-kami and Izawa Mimasaka-no-kami:

1 *Engetsutō; naginata* 偃月刀 [halberd; polearm with crescent-moon shape sword]

1 *Yari* 槍 [spear; lance]

2 *Tantō* 短刀 [short swords]

1 *Kagami* 鏡 [mirror]

1 *Shōshō; kogane* 小鐘 [small bell]

1 *Nukikae saiga shi* 抽替彩画笥 [painted, decorated clothes chest]

100 *Kamon mushiro* 華紋席 [straw mats decorated with floral design]

7 *Shi no [no] utsuwa; shi no utsuwamono; seika shiki* 青花瓷器 [Blue and white porcelain wares fashioned after the Ming Chinese wares]

1 *Suzuribako* 硯匣 [inkstone box; writing box]

1 *Kamibako* 紙匣 [stationery box]

1 *Tsukue* 机 [desk]

2 *Teishobako* 逓書函 [letter boxes]

1 [set] *Urushi-e kobako* 漆絵小箱 [large and small handy boxes lacquered dark red]

5 [bolts] *Kōketsu shūsha; beni shibori shūsha* 紅纐纈紗 [red crape de chine]

5 [bolts] *Shiketsu shūsha; murasaki shibori shūsha* 紫纐纈紗 [purple crape de chine]

100 *Amagasa* 雨傘 [umbrellas]

Reception Commissioners' Farewell Gifts

From Hayashi Daigaku-no-kashira:

2 *Kaiheki gafuku* 掛壁画幅 [picture scroll wall hangings]

2 [rolls] *Origane kinu* 織金絹 [brocade]

From Ido Tsushima-no-kami:

1 *Raden-bako* 螺鈿箱 [lacquer box with inlaid shell decoration]

From Izawa Mimasaka-no-kami:

2 *Kyōka* 鏡架 [mirrors with stands]

1 *Kamibako* 紙匣 [stationery box]

1 *Suzuribako* 硯匣 [inkstone box, writing box]

2 *Teishobako* 逓書函 [letter boxes]

From Udono Mimbe shōyu:

2 *Kaiheki gafuku* 掛壁画幅 [picture scroll wall hangings]

2 *Shuro* 手炉 [small brasiers; hand warmers]

---

* The original Japanese title is [*Ansei gannen*] *Gogatsu jūyokka Amerika ōsetsu-gakari yori Beijin e no sōhin mokuroku.*

IIIA. List of Official Ryūkyūan Gifts Presented at Naha on 8 June 1853

The source for this list is "Peri kantai Okinawa raikō kankei Satsuma-han Naha zai bugyō todokesho" [Reports of the Perry Squadron's Ryūkyū Visits by the Naha Magistrate Appointed by Satsuma *han*], in Hora, Tomio, 1970, *Peri Nihon ensei zuikō-ki,* page 482.

To the Commodore:

10 *sensu* 扇子 [folding fans]

4 [sets] *kinu tabako-ire kiseru-ire tsuki* 絹煙草入幾セル入付 [silk tobacco pouches and pipes]

2 *kin* [1.2 kg] *Kokubu tabako* 国分煙草 [Kokubu (district, Kagoshima prefecture) tobacco]

2 [sheaves] *shiro asa* 白麻 [white hemp]

3 *Sukiya tenugui* 数寄屋手拭 [tea (ceremony) towels]

1 *tan* [roll = 12 yards] *momen rinji nuno* 木綿りん地布 [pure, high quality cotton cloth]

1 [roll] *shiro saya* 白紗綾 [white figured silk]

1 [roll] *Tango jima* 丹後縞 [striped Tango (northern Kyoto) silk]

To the Captains of the *Susquehanna* and *Mississippi,* the translator, two other officers, and the Commodore's son, to each:

10 *sensu* 扇子 [folding fans]

4 [sets] *kinu tabako-ire kiseru-ire tsuki* 絹煙草入幾セル入付 [silk tobacco pouches and pipes]

2 *kin* [1.2 kg] *Kokubu tabako* 国分煙草 [Kokubu brand tobacco]

1 [sheaf] *shiro asa* 白麻 [white hemp]

1 [roll] *Mōka nuno* 眞岡布 [cotton fabric produced in Mōka, Tochigi prefecture]

IIB.   List of Official Ryūkyūan Gifts Presented to
the American Expedition Party at Naha on 11 July 1854

The source for this list is "Peri kantai Okinawa raikō kankei Satsuma han zai bugyō todokesho" [Reports of the Perry Squadron's Ryūkyū Visits by the Naha Magistrate Appointed by Satsuma *han*], in Hora, Tomio, 1970, *Peri Nihon ensei zuikō-ki,* pages 484–485.

[Recipient Unspecified]:

10 *sambon mono sensu* 三本物扇子 [three-rib folding fans used in the tea ceremony]

1 *soku* [bundle] *Sugihara gami* 杉原紙 [Sugihara (modern Hyōgo prefecture) paper treated with rice paste]

10 *tabako ire* 多葉紛入 [tobacco pouches]

10 *kiseru* 幾世留 [tobacco pipes]

5 *kin* [3 kg] *Kokubu tabako* 国分煙草 [Kokubu (district in Kagoshima) brand tobacco]

1 *bentō* 弁当 [lunch box]

2 [sets] *suzuri buta* 硯フタ [trays]

2 *meshibako* 飯箱 [rice (cooked rice) boxes]

5 [*goku*] *jō yaki* [*mono*] *choka* 極上焼物茶家 [high quality pottery tea jars]

3 *soku* [bundles] *dō chawan* 同茶椀 [high quality tea cups]

1 *dō mizu-sashi* 同水サシ [high quality ceramic water pitcher]

1 *dō chōji furo* 同丁子風炉 [high quality pottery incense burner]

1 *dō hana-ire* 同花入 [high quality ceramic flower vase]

1 *dō chōzu-bachi* 同手水鉢 [high quality large water jar]

3 [rolls] *bashō nuno* 芭蕉布 [banana cloth; abaca cloth]

3 [rolls] *konji momen nuno* 紺地木綿布 [indigo cotton cloth]

5 [rolls] *Mōka nuno* 眞岡布 [Mōka cotton cloth]

IIIc.   List of Official Ryūkyūan Gifts Presented to
Commodore Perry at Naha on 12 May 1853 [lunar calendar]

The source for this list is "Zen-kindai 2: Peri raikō kankei kiroku" [Pre-Modern Period, 2: Official Records of Perry's Ryūkyū Visits], *in* Okinawa-ken Okinawa shiryō hensanjo, editor, 1982, *Okinawa-ken shiryō* [Historical Documents Relating to Okinawa Prefecture], pages 414–415.

To the Commodore:

Sensu nijuppon 扇子二十本 [20 folding fans]

Sugihara gami nijitchō 杉原紙二十帖 [20 folios of Sugihara paper]

Tabako ire roku-gumi kiseru ire tsuki 煙草入六組きせる入付 [6 sets of tobacco pouches and pipes]

Mōka nuno santan 眞岡布三端 [3 rolls of Mōka type cotton cloth]

Someji shima momen nuno ittan 染地嶋木綿一端 [1 roll of colored, striped cotton cloth]

Konji shima momen ni-tan 紺地嶋木綿布二端 [2 rolls of striped indigo cotton cloth]

Aka shima nuno ni-tan 赤嶋布二端 [2 rolls of red-striped cloth]

Shira hoso [goku] jō nuno san-tan 白細 [極] 上布三端 [3 rolls of white, finely woven high quality cloth]

Tabako go-kin 煙草五斤 [5 *kin* (1 *kin* = 0.6 kg) tobacco]

Meshibako futatsu 飯箱二 [2 rice (cooked rice) boxes]

Suimonowan issoku 吸物椀一束 [1 bundle of soup bowls]

Bentō ittsū 弁当一通 [1 lunch box]

Shōchū futa-tsubo nijūgo-hai iri 焼酎二壺二十五盃入 [2 25-cup capacity jugs of rice wine]

IIID. List of Official Ryūkyūan Gifts Presented to Commodore Perry at Naha on 17 June 1854 [lunar calendar]

The source for this list is "Zen-kindai 2: Peri raikō kankei kiroku" [Pre-Modern Period, 2: Official Records of Perry's Ryūkyū Visits], *in* Okinawa-ken Okinawa shiryō hensanjo, editor, 1982, *Okinawa-ken shiryō* [Historical Documents Relating to Okinawa Prefecture], pages 543–544.

Sambon mono sensu nijuppon 三本物扇子弐拾本 [30 three-rib folding fans used in the tea ceremony]

Shiro asa go-soku 白麻五束 [30 sheaves of white hemp]

Sugihara-gami ni-soku 杉原紙弐束 [2 bundles of Sugihara paper]

Oribe-gata ginu tabako ire jūgo-kumi kiseru ire tsuki 折部形多絹葉紛入拾五組きせる入付 [15 sets of Oribe type silk tobacco pouches and pipes]

Kokubu tabako jukkin 国分多葉粉拾斤 [10 *kin* (1 *kin* = 0.6 kg) Kokubu tobacco]

[Goku] jō yaki [mono] chōji furo hitotsu ［極］上焼［物］丁子風爐壱ツ [1 high quality pottery incense burner]

Shunuri suimonowan ni-soku 6朱塗吸物椀二束 [2 bundles of red lacquer soup bowls]

Bentō ittsū 弁当壱通 [1 lunch box]

Suzuri buta ni-kumi 硯ふた弐組 [2 sets of trays]

Meshibako futatsu 飯箱弐ツ [2 rice (cooked rice) boxes]

[Goku] jō yaki [mono] choka itsutsu ［極］上焼［物」茶家五ツ [5 high quality pottery tea jars]

Dō chawan san-soku 同茶椀三束 [3 bundles of high quality tea cups]

Dō ambin futatsu 同阿ん遍ん弐ツ [2 high quality ceramic water pitchers]

Dō hanaire futatsu 同花入弐ツ[2 high quality ceramic flower vases]

Dō mizubachi futatsu 同水鉢弐ツ [2 high quality ceramic water jugs]

Bashō nuno san-tan 芭蕉布三反 [3 rolls of banana cloth]

Konji momen nuno san-tan 紺地木綿布三反 [3 rolls of indigo cotton cloth]

Shirobana saya ittan 白花紗綾壱反 [1 roll of white figured silk]

Mōka nuno go-tan 眞岡布五反 [5 rolls of Mōka type cotton cloth]

Jūshichi-sen [kasuri] kon shima nuno san-tan 拾七舛紺嶋布三反 [3 rolls of striped, splashed-patterned indigo cotton cloth]

IV. List of Articles Purchased by Dr. James Morrow

The source for this list is Allan B. Cole, editor, 1947, *A Scientist with Perry in Japan: The Journal of Dr. James Morrow*, pages 230–233.

List of Specimens in Arts Manufactures &c. Bought in Hakodadi Japan Lat. 42^1/$_2$°N

Foot Adze
5 Small files
1 Specimen dried tow
Small Hammer
2 Knives
2 small saws
Half inch Chisel
Three fourths inch Chisel
Six Tenths inch Chisel
Two Tenths inch Chisel
Three Tenths inch Chisel
Six Tenths inch Chisel
One Tenth inch Chisel
Four Tenths [inch] Gauge
Four Tenths [inch] Gouge (thick)
One inch & four tenths chisel
Two pair Brass Hinges
One pair iron Hinges
Two papers needles
One paper Brass tacks
Two iron Hooks
Two brass Handles
Four tweezers
Hooks & Staples
Paper black nails
Paper bright Hooks
Paper Spikes
Small spikes
Pair Steel yards for weighing
Large Whip saw
Large Iron Kettle
Two dippers
Small chisel
Two spindles
One Ink Stone
One pair Scissors
One Large bit for plane
Small Bit for plane
Trimming Knife chisel
3/4 inch chisel
Two planes
One Japanese lock
One small ripping saw

One drawing Knife
One Iron notched tea Kettle

List of cloths cotton silk & grass bought in Hakodadi

Diamond Spot
Blue Kerchief
Blue   " Spots
Two red Fancy Kerchiefs
Blue Stripe
Blue check
Black & white (variegated)
Thin white
Thick white
Black centre
Japanese printed Silk (dark colour)
Piece printed cloth gold stamp
Red & white fine silk
Blue & white plaid silk
Piece grass cloth (linen)
One piece cotton stripe
One piece fillagree
One Kerchief
One   "   Blue & white (fancy)
Blue cotton sash—
One piece Blue & white
One Striped cotton Sash
One fancy Yellow & green
Blue Transverse square
One piece printed cotton (peculiar)
One small piece (fancy)
Two small fancy

List of Specimens in Natural History arts Manufactures &c. bought in Simoda Japan 32^1/$_2$° Degrees [sic] N. Latitude & brought to the U.S.

3 Specimens fine bloome or iron ore
Specimen Copper ore
Specimen Lignite ore
Peculiar bullrush used as sand paper
Two large fish, for their skins
Specimens of Hemp
10 half quires of paper made of bark of tree *Morus popepea*
Ream of very fine ladies paper (same)
Iron pot
Coil Iron wire

Small copper wire
Whet-stones
Coil large copper wire
Tea Kettle
Ream of Japanese paper
Ginsing root
2 Farmers knives
Plough casting

Broad blunt Knife

June, Specimens copper ware & plate
Reaping Knife
Japanese Hoe
Spade
8 pots flowers
Three Household shrines

V. List of Articles Desired by the Americans, Submitted by the Reception Commissioners to the Rōjū [Senior Council] on 24 May 1854

The source for this list is "*Machi bugyō shoruisho shū gaikoku jiken sho*" [Shimoda City Magistrate Records Relating to Foreign Affairs], in *Bakumatsu gaikoku kankei monjo* [BGKM], 1914, volume 6, pages 197–202.

For the United States Government:

Nuri dansu 塗箪笥 [lacquered clothes chest]

Nuri handai kyokuroku 塗飯台曲録 [lacquered table and chair]

Tatami [*hana mushiro*] 畳 [花莚] [straw-woven, decorated floor mats]

Yakimono rui 焼物類 [pottery ware]

Tetsu narabi ni hagane mono 鉄並鋼物 [iron and other metalware]

Danjo ifuku 男女衣服 [men's and women's clothing]

Jūhi gyohi saiku mono 獣皮魚皮細工物 [animal hide and fishskin crafts]

Oyoso nijō nana shaku no Nihon-sen tadashi shogu o sou 凡弐丈七尺之日本船但諸具添 [fully rigged Japanese boat of approximately six meters in length and a beam of two meters]

Nihon buki 日本武器 [Japanese weapon]

Nihon-sen no hinagata 日本船の雛型 [models of Japanese ships]

Nihon gozafune no hinagata 日本御座船の雛型 [model of Japanese state barge]

Jumoku no nae 樹木の苗 [tree seedlings]

Kusabana no nae 草花の苗 [flower seedlings]

Chō, ju, kai rui 鳥獣貝類 [birds and shells]

Kempu chirimen karamushi mempu 絹布縮緬苧綿布 [crepe silks, ramie, and cotton fabrics]

For Commodore Perry [either as direct gifts or merchandise available to him for purchase]:

Gokujō nuri handai kyokuroku tansu 極上塗飯台曲録箪笥 [top quality lacquered table, chair, and clothes chest]

Tsukue bunko suzuri-bako 卓文庫硯箱 [stationery and ink-stone boxes]

Nihon hibachi 日本火鉢 [hibachi]

Nuri-bako 塗箱 [lacquered box]

Dō sarawan 同皿椀 [lacquered bowls]

Danjo no kyōdai 男女の鏡台 [men's and women's mirror with stand]

Nihon no gambutsu 日本の玩物 [Japanese toys]

Nihon kake-e [*keiga*] 日本掛画 [Japanese scroll painting wall hangings]

Bokuseki zaiku mono 木石細工物 [wood and stone crafts]

Nihon kempu chirimen sha 日本絹布縮緬紗 [Japanese *crepe de chine*]

Kago zaiku mono 籠細工物 [basketry]

Nihon tenuki 日本手貫 [Japanese gloves]

Nihon setta geta 日本雪駄下駄 [Japanese snow shoes and wooden clogs]

Nuri-gasa 塗笠 [lacquered hat]

Nihon-sen no hinagata 日本船の雛型 [models of Japanese ships]

Gyohi zaiku hitsu 魚皮細工櫃 [fishskin crafts]

Dō nurimono 銅塗物 [copper castware]

Tatami [*hana mushiro*] 畳 [花莚] [straw-woven floor mats decorated with floral design]

For Purchases by Others at Shimoda:

Nuri handai 塗飯台 [lacquered table]

Nurimono 塗物 [lacquerware]

Nuri-gasa 塗笠 [lacquered hat]

Dō nurimono rui 銅塗物類 [copper castware]

Aogai nurimono 青貝塗物 [mother-of-pearl inlay lacquerware]

Kami zaiku nurimono 紙細工塗物 [papier-mâché products]

Kempu ifuku 絹布衣服 [silk clothing]

Mino narabi ni tōyu gappa 蓑並銅 [桐] 油合羽 [oiled straw rain coat]

Yakimono chawan zara 焼物茶椀皿 [ceramic tea cups and plates]

Kago-tsumi yakimono 籠包焼物 [pottery with bamboo covering]

Kaisō okimono 海草置物 [sea grass ornamental figures]

Take zaiku narabi ni kyō [*tō*] *zaiku kago* 竹細工並喬 [籐] 細工籠 [bamboo baskets and other woven crafts]

Zenwan 膳椀 [serving bowls]

Kabin 花瓶 [flower vase]

Nihon kagami 日本鏡 [Japanese mirror]

Byōbu 屏風 [folding screen]

Kasa 傘 [umbrella]

Shōni gambutsu 小児玩物 [children's toys]

Sha chirimen kempu 紗縮緬絹布 [*crepe de chine*]

Nōgu no hinagata 農具の雛型 [samples of agricultural implements]

VI.   1953 Accession List: Division of Ethnology
List of Presents Given by the Emperor [sic] of Japan
to Commander [sic] Mathew [sic] C. Perry, March, 1859

The source for this list is the NMNH Registrar's Office, Accession File Number 199043

ECC No.	Item	ECC No.	Item
1	Japan Silk, Red	125–127	Japan China cups, white & blue
2	Japan Silk, Yellow	128–130	Japan China cups, dark blue
3–5	Japan Fan	131–133	Japan China cups, white
6–14	Wooden cup & saucer	134–135	Japan earthen little jars, dark
15	Wooden black bowl	136–148	Japan red wooden cups & saucers
16	Wooden brown bowl	149	Large & highly ornamented wooden teawaiter
17	Wooden black bowl	150	Mirror and case
18	Wooden black cup & saucer	151	Japan tea box
19	Wooden brown cup & saucer	152	Black working box
20	Wooden work box, black	153–155	Black pearl figd. boxes
21	Wooden work box, red	156–158	Wooden highly ornamented red bowls
22	Wooden fan	159–161	Japanese household gods
23–24	Wooden tea chest	162–163	Japanese tea apparatus boxes
25	Wooden fan	164–165	Bamboo water canteens
26	Japan red silk	166	Bamboo goblet
27	Japan belt	167–170	Japan shell spoons
28	Japan yellow silk	171–173	Japan earthen brown jars
29	Lew Chew pipes	174–175	Japan earthen brown jars, smaller size
30	Lew Chew pouches	176	Earthen brown little jar
31	Lew Chew pipe	177–182	Red wooden cups and saucers
32	Lew Chew pouch	183–188	White & blue china cups
35–43	Japan pipes	189–194	Dark blue china cups
44–45	Lew Chew tobacco	195–200	White small china cups
71	Fancy box gilt	201–206	Small transparent china cups
72	Segar writing case	207	Sword-like spear ornamented with scabbard
103–104	China large dish	208	Plain spear with scabbard
105	China cylinder water jar	209–231	Japan assortd. pieces of silk
106	China round water jar	232	Japan red pieces of silk
107	China butter pot	233	Japan white pieces of silk
108	China vegetable dish	234–255	Japan assortd. pieces of silk
109	Bamboo small basket	256	Japan white pieces of silk
110	Rattan working basket	257	Japan red pieces of silk
111	Tissue paper fan	258–262	Japan assortd. pieces of crape
112	Tissue paper, 1 ream	263	Japan white pieces of crape
115–116	Japan swords with scabbards	264–268	Japan assorted pieces of cotton cloth
117	Rattan working basket	269–271	Japan assorted pieces of grass
118	Fancy cane little table	272	Box Lew-Chew tobacco
119	Pouch	273	Japan gong
120	Pipe	273–275	Bamboo basket
121	Pouch	276	Rattan working basket
122	Pipe	277	3 dark rollers
123–124	Ladies cuffs of shaw	278	3 light rollers

148

ECC No.	Item	ECC No.	Item
279	6 reed	328	Iron wire
280	Paper fan	329–330	Copper wires
281	Cast-iron dinner pot	331	Copper holders
282	Earthen kettle	332	Iron holders
283	Cast-iron kettle	333	Iron-hat-hooks
284	Cast-iron teapot	334	Japan sand
285	Clay teapot	335–337	Brooms
286	Imitation cast ponkin	338–339	Pin cushion of light wood
287	Copper stew pan	340–345	Box of Japan shells
288	Cast-iron shovel	346	Japan iron hammer & handle, extra
289	Cast-iron ladle	347	Draw knife
290	8 paper fans	348	Whipsaw
291	Japan rolled paper	349–350	Japan compass small saws
292–296	Ladies' note fancy writing paper	351	Japan small saw
297–300	Japan writing paper	352	Japan needles, large
301	Japan sanctuary 1st class	353	Japan needles, 2nd size
302	Japan sanctuary 2nd class	354	Japan copper nails
303	Japan sanctuary 3rd class	355	Japan iron nails
304–306	Japan baby dolls	356	Japan brass and iron hinges
307–308	Five brooms	357	Japan plain
309	One broom	358	Japan plain, large size
310	2 thin copper sheets	359–363	Japan carpenters implements of chisels of different sizes
311	7 plates, 3 brushes, 1 mallet—printers implements	364	Japan carpenters implements of chisels, very small
312	Ink bottle, printer's implements	365–369	Japan carpenters implements of chisels, large
313	Japan inkstand	370–371	Japan plough bits
314	Japan writing brushes	372–373	Japan hones
315–316	Japan baby dolls	374	Japan hoe, large size
317	[cocoanut fiber]	375	Japan hoe, 2nd size
318	Table mats	376–377	Japan hoes
319	Large kitchen knife	378–379	Japan spades
320	Small kitchen knife	380	Japan cast-iron plough shear point
321	Lignite	381	Japan hand hoe for beans
322–324	Copper pan in lacquer stand	382–384	Chinese scythe for rice
325	Lacquered stool	385–388	Japan hand scythes
326	Large square porcelain tank, 2 holes in the bottom	389–445	Japan common umbrellas
327	Stink pot		

VII.   List of American Presents
Brought Ashore in Japan on 13 March 1854

The source for this list is Roger Pineau, editor, 1968, *The Japan Expedition 1852-1854: The Personal Journal of Commodore Matthew C. Perry,* page 233.

For the Emperor:

Miniature steam engine, 1/4 size, with track, tender, and car.
2 telegraph sets, with batteries, three miles of wire, gutta percha wire, and insulators.
1 Francis' copper lifeboat.
1 surfboat of copper.
Collection of agricultural implements.
Audubon's Birds, in nine vols.
Natural History of the State of New York, 16 vols.
Annals of Congress, 4 vols.
Laws and Documents of the State of New York.
Journal of the Senate and Assembly of New York.
Lighthouse Reports, 2 vols.
Bancroft's History of the United States, 4 vols.
Farmers' Guide, 2 vols.
1 series of United States Coast Survey Charts.
Morris *Engineering.*
Silver-topped dressing case.
8 yards scarlet broadcloth, and scarlet velvet.
Series of United States standard yard, gallon, bushel, balances and weights.
Quarter cask of Madeira.
Barrel of whiskey.
Box of champagne and cherry cordial and maraschino.
3 boxes of fine tea.
Maps of several states and four large lithographs.
Telescope and stand, in box.
Sheet-iron stove.
An assortment of fine perfumery.
5 Hall rifles.
3 Maynard muskets.
12 cavalry swords.
6 artillery swords.
1 carbine.
20 Army pistols in a box.
Catalogue of New York State Library and of Postoffices.
2 mail bags with padlocks.

For the Empress:

Flowered silk embroidered dress.
Toilet dressing-box gilded.
6 dozen assorted perfumery.

For Commissioner Hayashi:

Audubon's *Quadrupeds.*
4 yrds. scarlet broadcloth.
Clock.
Stove.
Rifle.
Set of Chinaware.
Teaset.
Revolver and powder.
2 dozen assorted perfumery.
20 gallons of whiskey.
1 sword.
3 boxes fine tea.
1 box of champagne.
1 box of finer tea.

For Abe, Prince of Ise, first councilor:

1 copper lifeboat.
Kendall *War in Mexico* and
    Ripley *History of the War in Mexico.*
1 box of champagne.
3 boxes fine tea.
20 gallons whiskey.
1 clock.
1 stove.
1 rifle.
1 sword.
1 revolver and powder.
2 dozen assorted perfumery.
4 yards scarlet broadcloth.

For each of the other five councilors:

1 book.*
10 gallons of whiskey.
1 lithograph.
1 clock.
1 revolver.
1 rifle.
1 sword.
12 assorted perfumery.

---

* The books thus distributed were Lossing, *Field Book of Revolution;* Owen, *Architecture, Documentary History of New York;* Downing, *Country Houses;* and Owen, *Geology of Minnesota.*

VIII.   List of American Presents to the Queen Dowager, Regent, and Treasurers of the Kingdom of Ryūkyū, and to Individual Japanese Officials

The source for this list is S. Wells Williams, 1910, *A Journal of the Perry Expedition to Japan (1853–1854)*, edited by F.W. Williams, pages 24, 67–68, 205, 244.

June 7–8, 1853, Naha, Ryūkyū

To the Queen Dowager:
  Looking glasses
  Soap
  Perfume, etc.

To Each of the Two Treasurers:
  1 engraved picture
  1 sword
  4 pieces of cotton
  1 bottle of whiskey
  1 bottle of wine
  1 cake

July 16, 1853, Edo Bay

To Kayama Eizaemon, Assistant Magistrate of Uraga:
  1 box of tea
  3 engravings of steamers and a house
  3 History of U.S.A.
  20 pieces of coarse cotton
  1 bale of drillings [a variety of American seeds]
  1 loaf of sugar

  1 box of champagne
  1 demijohn of whiskey

June 9, 1854, Shimoda

To the two new Reception Commissioners, Tsuzuki (Mineshige) Suruga-no-kami and Takenouchi Seitarō:
  Rifles, swords, perfumery, etc.

July 11, 1854, Naha, Ryūkyū

To the Regent:
  1 revolver
  1 flask of powder
  1 engraving of the Washington Monument
  All remaining agricultural implements

To 1st Treasurer:
  1 dressing table
  1 engraving

To each of the 2nd and 3rd Treasurers:
  1 lorgnette
  1 engraving

IX.   List of Japanese Personal Names

Abe Masahiro 阿部正弘	Ise-no-kami (Lord of Ise [modern Mie prefecture]); senior member of *shōgun*'s council
Aibara Isaburō 合原緒三郎	Assistant to the Uraga Magistrate
Fujiwara Kunimitsu 藤原国光	Daiku Emon-no-jō (official metal-worker of the Imperial Palace Guard; maker of the Ryūkyūan 1456 Gokoku-ji temple bell
Fujiwara Tadahiro 藤原忠広	Musashi-no daijō (official swordsmith of the Musashi district [modern Tokyo, parts of Saitama and Kanagawa prefectures]); 17th century Hizen [modern Saga prefecture] swordsmith
Hayashi Dōshun (1583–1657) 林道春	Confucian scholar, appointed 1st Secretary of the Tokugawa Shogunate in 1606
Hayashi Noboru (1799–1856) 林煒	Daigaku-no-kashira (Lord Rector of the University at Edo); chief reception commissioner
Hirayama Kenjirō 平山謙次郎	Public censor, Kanagawa district
Hiroshige I (1797–1858) 廣重一世	*Ukiyo-e* artist
Hiroshige II (1829–1869) 廣重二世	*Ukiyo-e* artist
Ido Satohiro (d. 1858) 井戸覚弘	Tsushima-no-kami (Lord of Tsushima [modern Nagasaki prefecture]); reception commissioner; magistrate of Shimoda (temporary appointment, 1854); also known as Iwanami-no-kami, temporary co-governor of Uraga, 1853
Iida Keinosuke 飯田敬之助	Coastal defense regiment commander, Uraga, March 1854
Imai Handayū 今井半太夫	Mid-19th century paper manufacturer in Atami [city]
Itarajiki 板良敷	Official interpreter, The Kingdom of Ryūkyū
Izawa Masayoshi 伊沢政義	Mimasaka-no-kami (Lord of Mimasaka [modern Okayama prefecture]); reception commissioner
Kayama Eizaemon 香山栄左衛門	Assistant magistrate of Uraga
Kiyoharu 清合	Ryūkyūan tobacco pipe maker
Kojima Matajirō 小嶋又次郎	Japanese shopkeeper and author and illustrator of *Commodore Perry's Expedition to Hakodate May 1854*
Kunitsuna (1805–1868) 国綱	*Ukiyo-e* artist
Matsuzaki Mitsutarō 松崎満太郎	Hayashi Noboru's secretary
Mera [Mura?] Taichiro	*Ukiyo-e* print censor
Moriyama Einosuke 森山栄之助	Chief official interpreter
Muragaki Norimasa 村垣範正 (1813–1880)	Awaji-no-kami (Lord of Awaji [modern Hyōgo prefecture]); senior member of the 1860 first Japanese Mission to the United States
Muramatsu	*Ukiyo-e* print censor
Namura Gohachirō 名村五八郎	Official interpreter
Rissai (1829–1869) 立斉	Pseudonym of Hiroshige II, *Ukiyo-e* artist
Shigenobu (1787–1832) 重宜	*Ukiyo-e* print artist
Shō Kō-kun 尚広勲	Regent, The Kingdom of Ryūkyū, 1853
Shō Tai-kyū Ō 尚泰久王	King Shō Tai-kyū, The Kingdom of Ryūkyū (reigned 1454–1461)

Sukehiro　助廣	Mid-17th century swordsmith of the Echizen district
Toda Shiei　戸田氏栄	Izu-no-kami (Lord of Izu [modern Shizuoka prefecture]); magistrate of Uraga
Toyokuni III (1786–1864)　豊国	*Ukiyo-e* artist; also known as Kunisada I
Tsuta Sukehiro　津田助広	17th century Echizen [modern Fukui prefecture] swordsmith
Tsujiya Yasubei	*Ukiyo-e* publisher
Udono Nagatoshi　鵜殿長鋭 (1808–1869)	Member of the Board of Revenue (title: *mimbu shōyū*); reception commissioner
Utagawa Kuniyoshi　歌川国芳 (1798–1861)	*Ukiyo-e* artist; also known as Ichiyūsai Kuniyoshi
Watanabe Shoyemon　渡辺庄衛門	*Ukiyo-e* print censor

Literature Cited

Blakemore, Frances
1978. *Japanese Design through Textile Patterns.* 272 pages. New York and Tokyo: Weatherhill.

Boger, H. Batterson
1964. *The Traditional Arts of Japan: A Complete Illustrated Guide.* 351 pages. New York: Crown Publishers.

Casal, U.S.
1961. *Shikki* [Japanese Art Lacquers]. 66 + 11 pages, plates 1–40. Tokyo: Sophia University.

Cole, Allan B., editor
1942. *With Perry in Japan: The Diary of Edward Yorke McCauley, Acting Master's Mate in Powhatan.* Princeton, New Jersey: Princeton University Press.
1947. *A Scientist with Perry in Japan: The Journal of Dr. James Morrow.* 307 pages. Chapel Hill, North Carolina: University of North Carolina Press.

Cort, Louise Alison
1979. *Shigaraki, Potters' Valley.* Tokyo, New York, San Francisco: Kodansha International, Ltd.

Culin, Stewart
1958. *Games of the Orient: Korea.* China; Japan; Rutland, Vermont; Tokyo: Charles E. Tuttle Company.

De Garis, Frederic
1947. *We Japanese.* Edited by Yamaguchi Shōzō, 2 volumes. Miyanoshita: Fujiya Hoteru Kabushiki Kaisha.

Densmore, Frances
1927. Handbook of the Collection of Musical Instruments in the U.S. National Museum. *United States National Museum Bulletin,* 136: 164 pages. Washington, D.C.

Dower, John W.
1971. *The Elements of Japanese Design: A Handbook of Family Crests, Heraldry and Symbolism.* 170 pages. New York and Tokyo: Walker/Weatherhill.

Edmunds, William
1934. *Pointers and Clues to the Subjects of Chinese and Japanese Art.* 725 pages. London: Sampson Low, Marston & Com., Ltd.

Endō, Takeshi
1971. *Nihon no min'gu, Japanese Folk Art and Design, 1: Machi* [Town]. 174 pages. Tokyo: Keiyūsha.

Gakuyō shobō Editorial Board (JI)
1962. *Japanese Interiors.* 88 pages. Tokyo: Gakuyō Shobō.

Garner, Sir Harry
1955. *Oriental Blue and White.* 86 pages, plates 1–100. London: Faber and Faber.

Goode, George Brown
1892. The Genesis of the National Museum. *U.S. National Museum Annual Report for 1891,* pages 273–380. Washington, D.C.

Graff, Henry F., editor
1952. *Bluejackets with Perry in Japan, the Diaries of Master's Mate J.R.C. Lewis of Macedonian and Cabin Boy W.B. Allen of Vandalia.* 181 pages. New York: New York Public Library.

Griffis, W.E.
1876. *The Mikado's Empire.* 625 pages. New York: Harper & Brothers, Publishers.
1890. *Matthew Calbraith Perry: A Typical American Naval Officer.* 450 pages. Boston and New York: Houghton, Mifflin and Company.

Gunsaulus, Helen C.
1922. *Japanese Collections (Frank W. Gunsaulus Hall).* Anthropology Leaflet, 3: 19 pages. Chicago: Field Museum of Natural History.

Harvard University (UD)
1942. *Ueda's daijiten: A Japanese Dictionary of Chinese Characters and Compounds.* 2596 pages. Cambridge, Massachusetts: Harvard University Press.

Hauge, Victor, and Takako Hauge
1978. *Folk Traditions in Japanese Art.* 272 pages. Tokyo: Kodansha International.

Hawks, Francis L.
1856. *Narrative of the Expedition of an American Squadron to the China Seas and Japan, Performed in the Years 1852, 1853, 1854, Under the Command of Commodore M.C. Perry, United States Navy, by Order of the Government of the United States.* 624 pages. New York: D. Appleton and Company.

Heine, William
1990. *With Perry to Japan, A Memoir by William Heine; Translated, with An Introduction and Annotations by Frederic Trautmann.* Honolulu: University of Hawaii Press. [Original Title: Reise un die Erde nach Japan.]

Hickman, Money, and Peter Fetchko
1977. *Japan Day by Day: An Exhibition Honoring Edward Sylvester Morse.* 198 pages. Salem, Massachusetts: Peabody Museum of Salem.

Hokama, Seikō
1961. Ryūkyū no bonshō ni tsuite [On Ryūkyūan Temple Bells]. In *Bunkazai yōran* [A Survey of the (Ryūkyūan) Cultural Properties]. Naha: Ryūkyū seifu bunkazai hogo iinkai.

Holme, Charles
1892. The Use of Bamboo in Japan. *Transactions and Proceedings of the Japan Society of London,* 1:23–48. London.

Hommel, Rudolph P.
1937. *China at Work.* 366 pages. New York: The John Day Company.

Hora, Tomio
1962. Kaikoku to Shimoda [The Opening of Japan and Shimoda]. In *Izu Shimoda* [(The Local History of) Shimoda], pages 677–753. Tokyo: Chihōshi Kenkyūjo.

Hora, Tomio, translator
1970. *Peri Nihon ensei zuikō-ki* [A Journal of the Perry Expedition to Japan (1853–1854) by S. Wells Williams, First Interpreter of the Expedition, edited by his son F.W. Williams, 1910]. 553 + 17 pages. Tokyo: Yūshodō Shoten. [Translated from English to Japanese.]

Hume, Ivor Noel
1976. *A Guide to Artifacts of Colonial America.* 323 pages. New York: Alfred A. Knopf.

Jackson, Albert, and David Day
1978. *Tools and How to Use Them: An Illustrated Encyclopedia.* 352 pages. New York: Alfred A. Knopf.

Janata, Alfred
1965. *Das Profil Japans.* 294 pages. Vienna: Museum für Volkerkunde.

Joya, Moku [Mock Joya]
1958. *Things Japanese.* 732 pages. Tokyo: Tokyo News Service, Ltd.

Kanai, Madoka, and Fujio Shimomura
1961. Volume 6: Man'en gannen kem-bei shisetsu kankei gaikoku shimbun kiji [Foreign Newspaper Articles Relating to the 1860 First Japanese Embassy to America]. *In* Nichi-bei Tsūshō Hyakunen Gyōji Un'eikai, editor, *Man'en gannen kem-bei shisetsu shiryō shūsei* [Historical Source Materials Relating to the 1860 First Japanese Embassy to America]. Tokyo: Kazama Shobō.

Katō, Tōkurō, editor
1972. *Genshoku tōki daijiten* [Illustrated Encyclopaedia of Ceramics]. 1037 pages. Kyoto and Tokyo: Tankōsha.

Kazusada, Tanaka, compiler
1920. *Man'en gannen kem-bei shisetsu zuroku* [Pictorials Relating to the First Japanese Embassy to America in 1860]. Unpaginated. Tokyo: Maruzen Kabushiki Kaisha.

Kerr, George H.
1958. *Okinawa: The History of an Island People*. 542 pages. Vermont and Tokyo: Charles E. Tuttle Company, Rutland.

Knapp, Josephine Hadley, and Esin Atil
1975. *Oriental Ceramics: The World's Great Collections*. The Freer Gallery, volume 10. Tokyo: Kodansha.

Kojima, Matajirō
1953. *Amerika ichijōsha* [Commodore Perry's Expedition to Hakodate, May 1854: A Private Account with Illustrations by Matajirō Kojima]. 2 volumes. [Volume 1 contains handwritten Japanese text and illustrations; volume 2 contains an English translation and printed Japanese text, translation by Alice Cheney.] Hakodate: The Hakodate Kyōdo Bunkakai.

Komatsu, Taishū
1975. *Nihon no bijutsu, Number 229: Shikkō* [Japanese Art, Number 229: Lacquer Crafts]. 94 pages. Tokyo: Shibundō.

Kurihara, Yasujirō
1901. *Kahyō kō* [On Shop Marks]. *Tokyo Jinrui Gakkai Zasshi* [The Journal of the Anthropological Society of Tokyo], 16:179, 186–192.

Lancaster, Clay
1963. *The Japanese Influence in America*. 292 pages. New York: Walton H. Rawls.

Lane, Richard
1978. *Images from the Floating World: The Japanese Prints*. 364 pages. Fribourg, Switzerland: Office du Livre.

Laufer, Bethold
1902. The Decorative Art of the Amur Tribes. *Memoirs from the American Museum of Natural History*, VII (Anthropology Series, VI): 86 pages. New York.

Maeda, Yoshimi, Haruo Misumi, and Takeo Minamoto
1977. *Okinawa bunka-shi jiten* [Dictionary of Ryūkūyan Cultural History]. 572 pages. Tokyo: Tokyōdō.

Matsushima, Seiichi, editor
1978. Hajimete deatta Amerika [The First Encounter with America]. *Yokohama*, special supplementary issue (November).

Miyoshi, Masao
1979. *As We Saw Them: The First Japanese Embassy to the United States (1860)*. 232 pages. Berkeley, Los Angeles, London: University of California Press.

Mori, Fusui, editor
1942. *Kurofune dansō* [Essays on *Kurofune* (Black Ship)]. 348 pages. Shimoda: Shimoda Bunka Kyōkai.

Mori, Noboru
1969. *Nihon no monyō bijutsu* [Design Patterns in Japanese Art]. 298 pages. Tokyo: Tokyo Bijutsu.

Mori, Yoshio
1969. *Peri to Shimoda kaikō* [Perry and the Opening of Shimoda Harbor]. 180 pages. Shimoda: Shimoda Shidankai.

Morison, Samuel Eliot
1967. *"Old Bruin" Commodore Matthew Calbraith Perry, 1794–1856*. 482 pages. Boston and Toronto: Little, Brown and Company.

Morse, Edward S.
1886. Japanese Homes and Their Surroundings. *Peabody Academy of Science Memoirs*, 2: 272 pages. Salem, Massachusetts.
1901. *Catalogue of the Morse Collection of Japanese Pottery*. 384 pages, 68 plates. Boston: Museum of Fine Arts.
1917. *Japan Day by Day*. 2 volumes. New York and Boston: Houghton Mifflin Company.

Nakano, Eisha, with Barbara B. Stephan
1982. *Japanese Stencil Dyeing: Paste-Resist Techniques*. 143 pages. New York and Tokyo: Weatherhill, Inc.

Nakayama, Seimo, editor
1969. *Ryūkyū-shi jiten* [An Historical Dictionary of the Ryūkyūs]. Naha: Bunkyō Tosho.

New York Herald
1860. June 4th issue, newspaper collection microfilm reel, number 2128. Library of Congress.

Newman, Alex, and Egerton Ryerson
1964. *Japanese Art: A Collector's Guide*. 146 pages. New York: A.S. Barnes and Co.

Nihon Dai-jiten Kankokai, editor (NKDJ)
1976. *Nihon kokugo daijiten* [Encyclopaedia of Japanese Language]. 20 volumes. Tokyo: Shōgakukan.

Noma, Seiroku
1974. Japanese Costume and Textile Arts. Translated by Armins Nikovskis. *The Heibonsha Survey of Japanese Art*, 168 pages. Tokyo: Heibonsha.

Okada, Yuzuru
1956. *Japanese Handicrafts*. 180 pages. Tokyo: Japan Travel Bureau.
1958. History of Japanese Textiles and Lacquer. *In* Tokyo National Museum, compiler, *Textiles and Lacquer*, pages 1–70. Tokyo: Tōto Shuppan Co., Ltd.

Okamura, Kichiemon
1964. *Zuroku Okinawa no kōgei* [Handicrafts of Okinawa: A Pictorial Record]. Japanese text, 143 pages; English text, 30 pages. Tokyo: Seidōsha Publishing Company.

Okinawa Taimususha, editor
1983. *Okinawa daihyakka jiten* [Encyclopaedia of Okinawa]. Naha: Okinawa Taimususha.

Okinawa-ken Okinawa shiryō hensanjo, editor
1982. Zen-kindai, 2: Peri raikō kankei kiroku [Pre-Modern Period, 2: Official Records of Perry's Ryūkyū Visits]. *In Okinawa-ken shiryō* [Historical Documents Relating to Okinawa Prefecture]. Naha: Okinawa-ken kyōiku iinkai.

Ōtsuki, Fumihiko
1932–1937. *Daigenkai* [The Great Sea of Words: Dictionary of the Japanese Language]. 5 volumes. Tokyo: Fuzambō.

Papinot, E.
1948. *Historical and Geographical Dictionary of Japan*. 842 pages. Ann Arbor: Overbeck Company, Publishers.

Perry, M.C.
1853. M.C. Perry letter of 5 September 1853, Macao, to the President of the United States. Located in the Henry E. Huntington Library, San Marino, California.
1855. M.C. Perry letter of 3 November 1855 to Assistant Secretary Spencer F. Baird, U.S. Explorations and Government Reports, 1852–60, Smithsonian Institution Archives, Record Unit 52.
1856. M.C. Perry Letters of 2 and 25 October 1856 to to Secretary Joseph Henry, U.S. Explorations and Government Reports, 1852–60, Smithsonian Institution Archives, Record Unit 52.

Piggott, Juliet
1969. *Japanese Mythology*. 141 pages. London, New York, Sydney, and Toronto: Paul Hamlyn.

Pineau, Roger, editor (PJL)
1968. *The Japan Expedition 1852–1854; The Personal Journal of Commodore Matthew C. Perry*. 241 pages. Washington, D.C.: Smithsonian Institution Press.

Rhees, William J.
1879. The Smithsonian Institution: Documents Relating to Its Origin and History. *Smithsonian Miscellaneous Collections*, 328: 73 pages. Washington, D.C.

Roberts, Laurence P.
1976. *A Dictionary of Japanese Artists; Painting, Sculpture, Ceramics, Prints, Lacquer*. 209 pages. New York: Weatherhill, Inc.

Robinson, B.W.
1961a. *The Arts of the Japanese Sword.* 95 pages, plates 1–100. London: Faber and Faber.
1961b. *Kuniyoshi.* 71 pages, plates 1–98. London: Her Majesty's Stationery Office.

Robinson, H. Russell
1969. *Japanese Arms and Armor.* 54 pages, color plates 1–29, black-and-white plates 1–112. New York: Crown Publisher, Inc.

Sadaharu, Okatomi, editor
1968. *Monyō no jiten* [Dictionary of Decorative Design]. Tokyo: Tokyōdō Shuppansha.

Sakanishi, Shio, editor
1968. *A Private Journal of John Glendy Sproston, U.S.N.* 128 pages. Tokyo: Sophia University.

Salwey, Charlotte M.
1894. *Fans of Japan.* 148 pages. London: Kegan Paul Trench, Trubner, & Co., Ltd.

Satow, Sir Earnest Mason
1905. *Japan 1853–1864, or Genji yume monogatari.* Tokyo: Naigai Shuppan Kyōkai. [Translation of Kaikoku Shidan (History of the Opening of Japan) by Baba Bun'ei.]

Sera, Yosuke, editor
1959. *Ko imari sometsuke zufu* [Old Imari Blue and White Porcelain]. Japanese text, 76 pages; English text, 38 pages. Kyoto: Heiandō Co.

Shively, Donald H.
1968. Bakufu versus Kabuki. *In* John W. Hall and Marius B. Jansen, editors, *Studies in the Institutional History of Early Modern Japan,* pages 231–261. Princeton: Princeton University Press.

Shugio, H., editor
1896. *Catalogue of a Collection of Oriental Objects Belonging To Thomas E. Waggaman of Washington, D.C.* 492 pages. New York: The De Vinne Press.

Sieboldt, P.F. Von
1973. *Manners and Customs of the Japanese in the Nineteenth Century.* 298 pages. Rutland, Vermont, and Tokyo: Charles E. Tuttle Company. [Originally published by Harper & Brothers, New York, 1841.]

Smithsonian Institution
1855–1860, 1878, 1882–1884. *Smithsonian Institution Annual Reports for 1854–1859, 1877, 1881–1883.* Washington, D.C.: Smithsonian Institution.

Smithsonian Institution (CCJWA)
1883. *Descriptive Catalogue of General Horace Capron's Collection of Specimens of Antique Japanese Works of Art, Temporarily Deposited in the U.S. National Museum.* 48 pages. Washington, D.C.: Smithsonian Institution.

Spaulding, J. Willett
1855. *The Japan Expedition; Japan and Around the World, an Account of Three Visits to the Japanese Empire.* 377 pages. New York: Redfield.

Speiden, William Jr.
1855. Journal of a Cruise in the U.S. Steam Frigate Mississippi [9 March 1852–16 February 1855]. The unpublished manuscript is in the files of the Naval Historical Foundation, Navy Yard, Washington, D.C.

Statler, Oliver
1963. *The Black Ship Scroll.* 80 pages. Published by John Weatherhill, Inc., for The Japan Society of San Francisco and New York.

Stitt, Irene
1974. *Japanese Ceramics of the Last 100 Years.* 214 pages. New York: Crown Publishers, Inc.

Strange, Edward
1906. *The Color Prints of Japan, An Appreciation and History.* 85 pages. New York: Charles Scribner's Sons.

Suzuki, Takashi
1958. *Hiroshige.* 22 pages. New York: Crown Publishers.

Swann, Peter C.
1958. *An Introduction to the Arts of Japan.* 216 pages. Oxford: Bron Cassirer.

Szczesniak, Boleslaw, editor
1962. *The Opening of Japan: A Diary of Discovery in the Far East, 1853–1856.* 453 pages. [The diary of George Henry Preble.] Norman: University of Oklahoma Press.

Tanaka, Toyotarō, editor
1970. [Exhibition catalog.] Nippon mingeikan [Japan Folkcrafts Museum]. Unpaginated, plates 1–60. Tokyo: Mampaku Nippon mingeikan shutten kyōgikai.

Taylor, Bayard
1859. *A Visit to India, China, and Japan in the Year 1853.* New York: G.P. Putnam.

Tokyo bijutsu kurabu seinen-kai, editor (BT)
1982. *Bijutsu techō.* [Handbook of (Japanese) Art.] 531 pages. Tokyo: Tokyo bijutsu kurabu.

Tokyo University Historiographical Institute (BGKM)
1912–1930. Bakumatsu gaikoku kankei monjo [Official Documents Relating to Foreign Relations during the Late Edo Period]. In *Dai Nihon komonjo* [Collection of Ancient Japanese Historical Documents], volumes 4–6, 8, supplement 1. Tokyo: Teikoku daigaku shiryō hensanjo.

Tomes, Robert
1857. *The Americans in Japan: An Abridgment of the Government Narrative of the U.S. Expedition to Japan, under Commodore Perry.* 415 pages. New York, London: D. Appleton & Co.

Tsuboi, Ryōhei
1970. *Nihon no bonshō* [Japanese Buddhist Temple Bells]. Tokyo: Kadokawa shoten.

Tuer, Andrew W.
1967. *Japanese Stencil Designs.* 112 pages. New York: Dover Publications, Inc.

United States Congress, Senate
1855. *Correspondence Relative to the Naval Expedition to Japan.* 83rd Congress, 2nd session, Executive Document number 34. [Message to the President of the United States, transmitting a report of the Secretary of the Navy (J.C. Dobbin) in compliance with a resolution of the Senate of December 6, 1854, calling for correspondence, etc., relative to the naval expedition to Japan.] Washington, D.C.: United States Government Printing Office.

Varden, John
Ms. Varden's Diary, 1857–1863, unpaginated, in John Varden Papers 1829–1863, Smithsonian Institution Archives, Record Unit 7063.

Wakayama, Hōmatsu
1967. *Kanagu jiten* [Dictionary of Metalware]. 657 pages. Tokyo: Yūzankaku shuppan kabushiki kaisha.

Williams, C.A.S.
1976. *Outlines of Chinese Symbolism and Art Motives.* 472 pages. New York: Dover Publications, Inc.

Williams, S. Wells
1910. A Journal of the Perry Expedition to Japan (1853–54), Edited by F.W. Williams. *Transactions of the Asiatic Society of Japan,* 38(2).

Yanagi, Sōetsu
1960. *Nippon mingeikan ten* [Exhibition of Folkcrafts from the Collection of Japan Folk Crafts Museum]. Unpaginated, plates 1–54. Tokyo: Nippon Mingeikan.

Young, Martie W.
1973. *Asian Art: A Collector's Selection.* 231 pages. Ithaca, New York: Herbert F. Johnson Museum of Art, Cornell University.
1977. *Far Eastern Art in Upstate New York.* 139 pages. Ithaca, New York: Herbert F. Johnson Museum of Art, Cornell University.

Yumoto, John M.
1958. *The Samurai Sword: A Handbook.* 191 pages. Rutland, Vermont, and Tokyo: Charles P. Tuttle Company.